STARTUPS THAT WORK

The 10 Critical Factors
That Will Make or Break
a New Company

Joel Kurtzman
AND Glenn Rifkin

PORTFOLIO

PORTFOLIO
Published by the Penguin Group
Penguin Group (USA) Inc., 375 Hudson Street,
New York, New York 10014, U.S.A.
Penguin Group (Canada), 90 Eglinton Avenue East, Suite 700,
Toronto, Ontario, Canada M4P 2Y3
(a division of Pearson Penguin Canada Inc.)
Penguin Books Ltd, 80 Strand, London WC2R 0RL, England
Penguin Ireland, 25 St. Stephen's Green, Dublin 2, Ireland
(a division of Penguin Books Ltd)
Penguin Books Australia Ltd, 250 Camberwell Road, Camberwell,
Victoria 3124, Australia
(a division of Pearson Australia Group Pty Ltd)
Penguin Books India Pvt Ltd, 11 Community Centre, Panchsheel Park,
New Delhi – 110 017, India
Penguin Group (NZ), Cnr Airborne and Rosedale Roads, Albany,
Auckland 1310, New Zealand
(a division of Pearson New Zealand Ltd)
Penguin Books (South Africa) (Pty) Ltd, 24 Sturdee Avenue,
Rosebank, Johannesburg 2196, South Africa

Penguin Books Ltd, Registered Offices:
80 Strand, London WC2R 0RL, England

First published in 2005 by Portfolio,
a member of Penguin Group (USA) Inc.

10 9 8 7 6 5 4 3 2 1

Copyright © Joel Kurtzman, 2005
All rights reserved

Charts and diagrams provided by PricewaterhouseCoopers

LIBRARY OF CONGRESS CATALOGING IN PUBLICATION DATA

Kurtzman, Joel.
    Startups that work : the 10 critical factors that will make or break a new company
    Glenn Rifkin.
        p.   cm.
    Includes index.
    ISBN 1-59184-102-X
    1. New business enterprises—Management.   I. Rifkin, Glenn.   II. Title.
    HD62.5.K874 2005
    658.1'1—dc22   2005041918

Printed in the United States of America
Designed by Joe Rutt

For Kaaren Kurtzman
an entrepreneur at heart and in spirit
—J. K.

For Ben, Cameron, and Laura
—G. R.

Contents

STARTUPS THAT WORK

One

———

The Art of Building Businesses from Scratch

STARTING COMPANIES

Every large and successful company was once a startup struggling to survive. Some of these successful companies were conceived in a flash of inspiration and planned on the back of a napkin in a coffee shop or coffee bar. Others took shape painstakingly over time in a basement or garage. Some startups arose out of pure frustration when a gifted man or woman working in a big but dumb company saw his or her best plans dashed one too many times. Some startups were created and then flourished overnight, while others achieved success only through a long series of painful fits and starts. The point is, every company that exists today began rather small.

Only a small percentage of startups succeed. But how do you define success? You can look at the mom-and-pop pizza joint at the center of town to sift out a few clues (after all, it still exists even after facing an onslaught from all those national chains) or you can look at all those national chains, since they were startups too. Success is never uniform; it exists in a number of different forms. Simply surviving occupies the lowest rung.

Despite all the programs offered at all the colleges, universities, and business schools, despite small business administration loans, the odds still favor failure by a wide margin. And despite all the knowledge gained from family, angel, and venture-fund investors, the chances of backing a winner—a company that creates value over the long haul—still remains slim.

And yet, as a nation, as a people, we are addicted to the highs (and lows) of creating startups. Only Israel, Sweden, and Finland share our entrepreneurial zeal in any meaningful way. The rest of the world favors economic security and big company benefits over the rush of building a business from scratch.

As a nation and a people we have profited handsomely from the swagger and drive of successful entrepreneurs. Not only have they created wealth in abundance but they also are the country's job creation and innovation engines. Startups have improved our lives, changed the world, and kept the economy growing. They have made their founders and investors rich, and they have done these things despite the odds.

Startups are very disparate, and yet they also have many factors in common across industries and even eras. One can only wonder what the impact would be if the odds moved a percentage point or two in favor of startups.

With so much money and time riding on startups, a few questions come to mind:

- What factors are most responsible for a startup's success?

- What differentiates a successful startup from one that fizzles and dies?

- How important are factors such as boards of directors, seasoned management, cutting-edge technology, marketing and business models?

- What do we mean by "lasting value"?

- How do venture investors help or hinder startups?

- Are there important differences between venture-funded startups and those that bootstrap their way to success?

- How important is leadership for startups?

- How important is technology?

- In sum, why do startups succeed?

To answer these and other questions about startups in ways that can help entrepreneurs and investors increase their chances for success requires a disciplined and diligent approach.

Perhaps it is my own bias toward research, but in my view, "gut" feelings and "experience" offer little in the way of best practices that can be reproduced. And since so few of even the so-called savviest of investors have a success rate of even 15 percent (with success defined as the creation of lasting value, measured in ways that will be described later), any approach that relies upon individual testimony *alone* will have its limitations.

Because individual testimony is limited, for the purposes of this book we have utilized two different and complementary research methodologies to study startup companies over a period of about four years.

The research methodology (which will be described later) was designed to collect aggregate data as well as capture relevant individual experiences in a systematic way. The aim of this dual approach is to produce a compendium of meaningful research results that can be used to increase the chances of success for entrepreneurs and investors. Rather than theory, the inclination of this book is toward practice.

This is not to say that the conclusions in this book will help everyone. A bad idea for a business will always be, well, a bad idea. In addition, if an entrepreneur does a poor job at executing even a good idea, his or her results are likely to be suboptimal.

But for an entrepreneur with a good idea and a good sense of how to execute, this book is designed to *increase* the chances of success.

If you take as a starting point the 1980s, it is possible to recall a myriad of good to excellent entrepreneurial ideas that did not stand the test of time. In the personal computer field alone, a lot of companies attracted a lot of venture cash. For example, Alto, Altair, Atari, Commodore, Franklin, and Osborne (among many others) were companies with great products but brief lives. Each of these companies—for at least a few months or even longer—produced the best products available in a market that was rapidly expanding. For days to months, these companies were everybody's darlings as their founders graced the pages of newspapers and business magazines.

So why did these companies die? There are many reasons, but the most important reason was simply that some other company did what they did—only *better*. Some other company, looking at the same market, figured out how to exploit that market more fully and for the longer term. Learning how successful startups achieved their goals has been the emphasis of our research.

A TWO-TRACK RESEARCH APPROACH

There are two streams of research that support the conclusions in this book. The first entailed assembling a team of analysts to study a large selection of startups that created value during one of the most impossible periods for new businesses, 1999 through 2001. The team I assembled was made up of several analysts from PricewaterhouseCoopers' (PwC) Global Technology Centers in California, and in Europe, led by Mike Katz. It also included a group of statisticians from PwC's Belfast, Northern Ireland, survey unit, which was led by Colin McIlheney. In addition, the team included two seasoned outside analysts with significant venture capital and high-tech experience. The outside experts were

Peter Rothstein, of Allegro Ventures, and Eric Ingersoll, CEO of Mechanology, a startup in Attleboro, Massachusetts.

In this phase of our research, the team studied 350 successful startups in the United States, Europe, and Israel, and subjected all of them to the same rigid set of questions and analysis. Each of these companies was looked at more than once. The first batch of 350 companies was examined in 2001, then again in 2002, with a number of them looked at subsequently in 2003 and in 2004. During each research period some of the original companies failed. In 2001, there were 350 companies in the study; in 2002, it dwindled to 328 surviving companies, with about 300 still going strong at the time of the writing of this book. During each major phase of this study, the surviving companies increased their values or valuations and—if they needed it—were able to raise money to stay in business.

In addition to this stream of research, beginning in 2003, and continuing through late 2004, Glenn Rifkin, my longtime collaborator and friend, and I conducted dozens of in-depth, highly structured interviews with venture capital investors, angel investors, CEOs, and other executives and members of the boards of directors of startup companies. In addition, we interviewed executives from startups that had matured out of the startup phase. Several of those that succeeded did so by being acquired. Others succeeded through an initial public offering. Some of those that had succeeded faced setbacks, but all of the companies we looked at that had achieved some sort of "exit" survived.

Using these interviews as our base, we pieced together a number of very detailed case studies of successful startups and compared and contrasted those cases with others from companies that had succeeded or failed. Some of these case studies are included in this book; others, for reasons of space, brevity, and confidentiality, we simply collected and have used to inform our conclusions.

Advantages of This Approach

The advantage of taking a dual research approach is significant when compared with those that rely either on case studies alone or empirical research. First, our foundational study of 350 companies gives us a database of quantifiable characteristics that we can use to create maps that measure a company's attributes. Looking at those same companies over time taught us as much about our maps as about the companies. As a result, we were able to adjust our conceptual model of what works and what does not.

By understanding statistically what works and by researching companies in the aggregate in what is one of the largest studies of startups ever conducted, we began to gain a deeper understanding of the levers that can be pulled by investors, boards, executives, and managers in order to improve a startup's chances of success.

But statistics alone provide only so much information and very little nuance. Statistics are far more biased toward the "why" and are far less useful with regard to the "how." In addition, statistics by definition do not capture the critical human dimension since they are designed to remove individual variations from the mix in order to offer a portrait of the group.

In my own view, business is about people first, and everything else second. Strategies, processes, structures, and systems are only as good as the people implementing them. Good ideas never succeed on their own. For companies to prosper, there must be leadership, vision, and good working relationships inside the company. For companies to succeed, a direction must be set with everyone working together to achieve it. Nothing kills companies faster than dissent at the top.

People matter, and the individual contributions that people make do not come across when you are dealing strictly with data. For that reason, we also studied companies one on one. This is particularly true with regard to the role of leadership.

The task of senior management is to make certain that everyone works in concert to insure that their companies grow. To do so requires vision, insight, experience, and force of personality. To do that requires holding people accountable while delegating the right level of authority. To do that requires that one eye is always trained on the financial and product markets and the other on building the team. To do that requires that every day everybody in the company renews their commitment to the company's success. These are intensely human issues.

Furthermore, senior management must create an environment in which everyone understands what they have to do to create value.

Boards and board members also have a similar role. The first priority of a board is to help companies grow using whatever personal means they have at their disposal. When choosing who to put on a board—especially the board of a startup—the primary question to ask is: Can that person add value to the company through his or her personal connections and skills? The second priority for choosing a board member should be: Can that person hold senior management accountable for reaching their growth and profitability targets? Can they motivate executives to achieve higher levels of success? The third priority for choosing a board member is to select people who can act as watchdogs to protect the company and its investors from managers that spend too much or too freely in pursuit of their goals and to protect the investors from managers that fail to achieve those goals. Many companies, especially early-stage companies, have assumed these priorities for their boards, but in reverse order.

Each of the issues just mentioned are human issues, which means their peculiarities will not be discovered in an empirical study. Just the reverse. A large-scale study of companies is likely to smooth over behaviors that lie outside the norm, whether those behaviors are good or bad, value creating or value destroying.

To add back the human dimension, we conducted our interviews specifically to capture any of the so-called human factors that our empirical research might have ignored or missed.

To develop our interview frameworks, we used the conclusions of the empirical study, but we also informed it by interviewing experts, portions of which are featured in this book. Since Glenn and I have more than fifty years of combined experience observing companies, we also put our practiced eyes to the test. The result, we believe, is an analysis that has depth, but more importantly can shed light on how to improve your chances of success when starting or investing in a new company.

COMPLICATED NEWBORNS

While startups are not as complex as established companies with multiple business units, divisional structures, and hundreds or even thousands of employees, they are often more *complicated* to run. They are difficult because whereas a large corporation might reassess its strategy on an annual basis and its structure every couple of years, a startup is a work in progress with every element of the company in play on a real-time basis. And whereas large companies often play a game of defense designed to protect their markets and market share—sometimes at any cost—startups almost always play offense as they attempt to gain a foothold that is usually on someone else's turf.

What this means is that though the terms CEO and senior manager are used without distinction and applied to leaders of large and small businesses, the skills needed to be successful in one may not be transferable to the other.

Nowhere is this more evident than in the world's technology companies. Rod Canion, founder of Compaq Computer, wrote the business plan, raised the money, hired a management team, and took the company public in one of the most successful initial public offerings of the 1980s. But when Compaq became a large company, he proved to be the wrong man for the job. His backers ousted him.

While Michael Dell, founder of Dell Computer, the world's number-one personal computer maker, keeps the title of chairman, he has always had a very strong and very experienced chief operating officer running the company on a day-to-day basis. In fact, when the company foundered in the mid-90s, Dell hired Morton Topfer, a seasoned veteran from Motorola with decades of big-company operating experience, to turn the company around. When Microsoft became the world's most valued company and a large and diversified firm, Bill Gates, its cofounder, replaced himself as CEO with his good friend Steve Ballmer.

Successful founder-CEOs and big-company CEOs are just different. One critical difference between them is that CEOs of startups need higher levels of flexibility than leaders of established firms. Many CEOs of startups are serial entrepreneurs, whereas CEOs of established companies usually spend decades at the same company, slowly and carefully working their way up.

Steve Jobs is a case in point. Together with Steven Wozniak, Jobs started Apple Computer. When Jobs was ousted from that job, he went on to start Next Computing, which made snazzy, high-powered workstations. When Next Computing failed, Jobs started Pixar Animation, before returning to Apple as CEO. While far more successful than most entrepreneurial CEOs, Jobs's experience is hardly unique. As a breed, people like Jobs just like to start things. In fact, many entrepreneurial CEOs say they simply get bored with the more mundane chores like managing for the longer term. And rather than play the big-company defensive game of protecting market share, entrepreneurial CEOs love the thrill of attack.

These differences might simply be interesting curiosities if they did not require different types of leaders and leadership styles. As Eric Ingersoll observed as we began to examine the results of the empirical study, the game plan for established company leaders is to "promulgate and harvest" new ideas and then to put them to work.

People running startups, however, have a different task. Rather than promulgate and harvest, their job is to "filter and sift," since they are exposed to (some would say bombarded with) so much information about so many elements of their business on such a constant basis. In a startup, everyone has an answer—or many answers—whether or not there are questions. In a startup, investors are not kept at bay. They are in your face and on your board—and they are far from the patient types that read Graham and Dodd.

To do their jobs correctly and profitably, CEOs and other leaders in startups have to be able to dismiss ideas that are not pragmatic. But they also have to be quick to employ new ideas that are capable of producing results. They have to be what Nitin Nohria, of the Harvard Business School, calls *bicoleurs*, people who do what works, no matter what it takes.

As we learned in the 1990s, startups consume capital the way rockets consume fuel, which is one reason they call it the "burn rate." But the burn rate of a startup is only one element in the equation.

SPEED VERSUS PERFECTION

Since startups, unlike mature companies, do not begin each week with a menu of product and service offerings that can be sold, each delay in a product launch not only adds to the burn rate cost but also brings with it lost revenue. And while burn rate and lost revenue are conceptually different, the best CEOs view the two together. For that reason, whereas the leader of a large company can promote quality over speed, CEOs of successful startups are usually promoting speed over quality. Their minds are programmed to ask, on a constant basis, what's the quickest route to revenue? What's the quickest route to profitability?

In the 1990s, it became all too evident that too few entrepreneurial CEOs were asking these two questions. As a result, many companies armed with good ideas perished because they took too long to produce revenue. When that happened, venture and angel investors lost interest in these companies. Rather than provide more investment, investors pulled the plug. Those hit hardest by these decisions were the so-called perfectionist CEOs: those who for the most part valued quality over speed and great design over a quick product launch.

Our research and case studies indicate that aside from just a few obvious areas where perfectionism really does matter (mostly in the area of pharmaceutical products and medical devices), a perfectionist bent can be fatal to newborn companies. For this reason, entrepreneurial executives must understand how to create the right balance between the zealots in the backroom who are building the company's products and creating its services, and its salespeople who just want something to sell.

If perfectionism really did matter, the computer and software industries would never have gotten off the ground. If perfection really did matter, none of us would have heard the qualification "version 1.0 will be followed immediately by version 1.1," or, "downloadable patches will be available for our software in a few weeks time," or "this product will be followed by a free updated version with new security features." In other words, *speed trumps perfection almost every time.*

Because speed does trump perfection, the tensions in a startup are often quite different from those in a big company. If GM was to produce a car with as many flaws as most new software, it would be plagued with lawsuits. If Boeing or Airbus put new planes into service that required as many "fixes" as each new version of Windows, flying would still be a daredevil sport. Because big companies face big liabilities—and because they are more likely to defend a market rather than invent or attack a new one—large companies tend to be far more conservative than startups.

For boards seeking to hire a CEO, or for investors who want to back one, these differences make it very difficult to find the right person for the job. How do you find a person with strong operational experience who is also bold? How do you find someone who is bold and also knows how to coach people to work harder, longer, smarter in the face of adversity and zero revenue? How do you find an experienced manager who really understands that perfectionism is a trait that benefits a mature company but sinks new ones? How do you find a leader who enjoys eating pizza with the troops more than flying around in a corporate jet? How do you find someone who can keep everyone focused on the future?

There is more to leading a startup than understanding viscerally that speed trumps perfection. Leaders of small companies have to motivate their troops using different tools from those that work in mature companies. Leading a large company requires, among other things, executives who are adept at cutting costs while increasing levels of quality. Leadership also requires executives who can grow their companies at sustainable rates while inculcating in their employees a consistent set of values. It requires having an abiding faith that progress comes in a rapid succession of small steps. It also requires managing people who often value security more than risk taking and innovation.

For leaders of big companies, vision is not always part of the job specifications. Lou Gerstner famously taught that lesson when he took over as CEO of IBM. When Gerstner took the helm of the company, he told analysts, reporters, and anyone else who would listen that before creating a new vision for the company he had to focus on getting a lot of little things right. More recently, Admiral William Owens, CEO of Nortel Networks, reminded us that vision is less important than stemming a company's losses while you reenergize its morale.

CEOs of big companies that are able to keep the doors open, the lights on, and the troops fed can feel confident. CEOs of big companies that see their share price appreciate, their markets grow, and their profits rise do not also need the gift of prophecy to feel proud.

Startups, on the other hand, are all about vision, all about hope, all about the future. Because each employee at a startup begins with a blank slate, it is up to the CEO of that startup to create the picture. According to our research and case studies, the most important task for executives at startups is to hire the best, most talented people and to form them into teams. That is especially true because most investors consider management, or human, talent as the most important criteria for making an investment. Time and again we have heard from investors, "I didn't really understand the technology the company was developing, but I invested because I respected the CEO and the management team he was able to attract."

To lure the best talent, CEOs of startups need to entice talented people by showing them what is possible, not *what is*. CEOs must share their dreams and enthusiasm. But they also must share their networks, because among their other tasks CEOs of startups are also their company's CRO—"chief recruitment officer."

Time and again, when we interviewed people working in startups, they explained that the reason they joined the team was that they wanted to work with the CEO—who in many instances they had worked with or known before—and because they wanted to have a chance to "join with a world-class team." To lure the best and most talented people, CEOs must be able to communicate their vision for the future and make everyone understand that that vision can be achieved.

For all of the above reasons, few CEOs of startups are able to continue running their companies once they grow big. Sometimes the founder's presence looms so large that people don't really recognize that someone else—someone a little less visionary, a little less "edgy," and a lot more professional—is actually running the show. Walt Disney started the company that bears his name, but his brother Roy Disney ran it. And, as already noted, other successful founder-CEOs have created ways to stay on board—if they really want to, and most do not—as the resident visionary, while someone else takes over the day-to-day task of managing.

Even so, leaders of startups must possess a multitude of strengths, as uncovered in the twin research that underpins this book. For example, leadership at a startup requires:

- A vision for the company and a sense of its ultimate "size and shape"

- An understanding of business models and how to build and rebuild them

- A deep grasp of markets combined with the ability to "sell"

- A willingness to share power, rather than hoard it

- An almost "intuitive" knowledge of people, their strengths and weaknesses, and how well they will do as members of a team

- The power not only to motivate but also to keep small teams focused, *no matter what else fights for their attention*

- The ability to make investors feel confident, even when there are significant setbacks

- The power to transform directors from passive watchdogs into active value creators

- A jazz artist's improvisational ability

GROWING IN THE RIGHT WAY

In studying successful startups and contrasting them with those that failed, our research team developed a model regarding what matters most. The three essential subdivisions of this model are strategy, resources, and performance.

These three subdivisions are further broken down as follows:

- *Strategy,* which includes market size, competitiveness position vis-à-vis other companies, and the business model

- *Resources,* which includes cash and cash flow, value contributed by the investors (financial, expertise, and other contributions as well), and the management team and its ability

- *Performance,* which includes product development, sales and distribution channels, and the ability to acquire customers, especially the *right* customers through marketing and other means

(There are more subdivisions possible given our database of research, and they are utilized as needed to further develop our findings.)

These divisions and subdivisions equal roughly nine elements that the research team plotted. In order to do so in a way that was immediately visible, these plots became what we called "Star Charts," which, as you can see below, take the nine areas of research and dig even deeper. We used these star charts for our diagnostics and as a way in which to frame our assumptions.

The chart below, for instance, has twelve subdivisions, with the size and shape of the center "spike" indicating the relative robustness of each featured item under consideration. As a result, the so-called star shape at the center of each of these circles indicates where a company's strengths and weaknesses lie. The longer each arm of the star, the more robust that function; the shorter the arm, the less developed that function. When it comes to Star Charts, size does matter.

I am displaying an example of the charts here not because I want to subject the reader to this type of measurement system (they can be found in the appendix at the end of the book) but to

A Typical Star Chart for a Typical Company

Source: PricewaterhouseCoopers

demonstrate the analytics we used. In the above indicated chart, the sizes of the arms indicate the level of development of each function. In the hypothetical company illustrated by the Star Chart, it is well developed when it comes to penetrating the market, and it has a fair value proposition for obtaining return on its investment. It also must confront moderate barriers to entry. But what the chart also indicates is that the company has very little strength when it comes to developing customers, is weak with respect to forming channel and other distribution alliances, and is vulnerable to competition.

These charts are not meant as criticism—just the opposite. They are meant as maps. By creating maps that coolly point out a young company's strengths and weaknesses, investors, board members, executives, and managers can see what they must do to increase their chances of success.

Star Charts were created for each of the companies we studied. As such, they provided our research team with visual maps that demonstrated three things: First, a company's attributes can be mapped, in real time, as that company grows. Second, maps can be created to show investors how the management of their companies is doing. A Star Chart created *today* that captures a company's weaknesses should indicate, when the next chart is prepared, whether those weaknesses have been addressed. And third, these charts show that not all successful companies need to have the same Star Chart *shape*. What this point means in practice is that companies with different strategies for creating value require different strengths to do it.

The shape of the Star Chart also relates to the exit strategy each company decides to follow. While we learned that it is dangerous for young companies to focus too much on their exits—they instead need to concentrate on creating value—at some point in their life cycles the question of exit will arise. When it does, the Star Chart can be used to determine if they are on course. For example, the charts indicate that a company whose game plan is to build a full-service company and then exit by raising money in an initial public offering is likely to have a different profile from one that aims to merge with a rival or sell itself to a larger player. Companies whose investors want to exit using an IPO will want to see each arm of their Star Charts very well developed. Companies whose exit strategy means selling themselves to a larger firm will not need to develop each arm of their charts. By measuring each arm of the star, companies can plot their chances of success against their exit strategies.

This has profound implications. In effect, it says that the most important way to increase a company's chances for success is to set a strategic course at the beginning that will take it to an achievable endpoint. What this means in practice is that a strategy that says, "We want to be the number-one supplier of digital video cameras to the TV and movie industries," is far from sufficient. The strategy must also say, "We will achieve our goal by developing patentable technology that will make us a high priority acquisition target for an electronics giant like Sony." A strategy that is developed in such a way can be followed and its progress mapped. It also will help a company's leaders apply themselves and their resources efficiently. For example, it makes no sense to build sales, marketing, and distribution departments if the goal is to become part of Sony.

A company like Akamai, a Web services provider based in Cambridge, Massachusetts, which we both researched in the empirical study and dissected in the case studies, wanted to become a public company. Not only did an independent strategy match the company's Web services business model, the company's founders also believed the promise of an IPO would be the best way to attract investment capital.

If a company wants to develop as a stand-alone operation, independent and growing of its own accord, the charts it will produce should be filled out roughly equally along every access. The reason for that is straightforward: public companies need to be independent and they need to do everything well.

What this shows is that Star Charts for a company like Akamai would be very different from the chart for another company with another strategy. Even more important, what these differences underscore is the fact that the world's most successful startups are those that understand from the outset where they want to go.

WHAT WE MEAN BY VALUE

As you read this book and examine its conclusions, you will see that our basic metric of success is a company's ability to create value.

But what do we mean by value?

For the purposes of our research, we defined value creation very simply. In the empirical study, the ability to create value means that a company must have increased its net valuation after each round of financing. For example, if a company is valued at $5 million in its first round of financing, receives another $5 million in new financing in its second round of financing, and is then worth $10 million, we would conclude that the company had not created any value. For a company to create value, it must be worth significantly more than the amount of money it has received.

While valuing startups is often difficult, it is by no means magic. A company increases its value when those that evaluate its worth—bankers, accountants, investors, and so on—see that its products have value in the marketplace that will lead to revenue and a clearly defined path to profitability. Innovative patents that might not produce revenue today could be regarded as valuable if it was clear that they would produce value tomorrow. Similarly, assembling a world-class science team might be viewed as valuable if they have strong reputations.

People who place bets on companies are not thoughtless. They look at intellectual capital, the quality of management, and they recognize that these have worth. They also recognize that putting together a great team is no mean feat. As a result, the simple act of creating a company is sometimes viewed by investors as an act of value creation. This is especially true with regard to companies whose aim is to be acquired. In addition, value creation comes from something very basic: showing revenues increasing faster than expenses.

TALKING TO CEOS

In the first phase of our research, the team and I painstakingly developed a universe of more than 500 successful startup companies. The Belfast Northern Ireland statistical team called each of these companies and made appointments to speak with the CEOs of each of the companies. Because not every company the team called wanted to participate, we ended up with a universe of 350 companies that participated in the study.

The questions we asked each CEO proved both that they had endurance and that our interview team had stamina. We asked each of the 350 CEOs, for example, how many sources of funding they had sought out before they had finally lined up their first investors. We asked these CEOs to rate the strength of their management teams and to tell us about the barriers to entry they needed to overcome. We asked these CEOs to rate their technologies, if they were high-tech companies, and to compare their technology to what was available from other firms in the market. We asked each CEO to talk about their sales and marketing methods. We asked them to discuss the pluses and minuses of their business models and to describe the products and services they were developing. Each interview took about an hour to complete.

We were surprised by a great deal of what we learned. For example, even in the high-tech and software sectors, success is less dependent on technology than on having a great management team. We also learned, as we dissected these companies and studied what they told us, that venture capital investors tended to be less helpful than might otherwise be expected. This comment was repeated in a majority of the interviews we conducted. A large number of CEOs said their venture capital investors rarely offered useful guidance. Many complained they missed board meetings, rarely contributed to strategic discussions about the company's future, and when they did focus they spent most of their time looking at the finances of the companies in which they invested and not at the plans.

But not all of the insights offered by the CEOs we talked to contained complaints. We were happily surprised by how much attention these CEOs paid to the market. Again and again we heard from these CEOs that they wanted to build their companies around their customers' needs. Many of the most insightful CEOs talked about how they used customers—or future customers—as sounding boards as they built their companies.

In a few instances, having such an intense focus on the market led to problems. In our case studies we discerned that CEOs and their technical teams were often at odds over where to put resources—in marketing or in technology. The CEOs we studied were generally biased toward the market and marketing and were persuaded that new technology and other types of innovations could achieve successful results if they were incrementally applied. Among CEOs there was a reluctance to base the company solely around a new technology. They told us that if you make technology the focus—and that technology is late—you may miss the mark entirely. As a result, they told us that relying on new technology alone is simply too risky a strategy.

The emphasis CEOs put on marketing was something of a surprise. We did not expect to see as much riding on the marketing function as we did, especially in the case studies. Marketing is often a company's forgotten stepchild. But marketing combined with a well thought through approach to sales and channel management is profoundly important. Even more important, as study participant Peter Rothstein observed when he examined the data, "customer acquisition is important, but what is more important is acquiring the right customers."

What this means for startups is that customers are not enough. You need those that champion your products or services to others. You need customers that see you as strategic to their business needs.

Obviously, the best customers are those that have powerful channels themselves for reselling your wares. Creating a customer out of a large technology consulting firm is vital if you are in the software business. Having a customer like Best Buy is vital if you are selling consumer technology. In other words, choosing the right customers is important for the long-term viability of a startup. Having the wrong customers, even though they might provide revenue, can be deadly since they can consume too much time, which is the scarcest resource of all for a startup.

There are many important findings in the research for this book that we have uncovered and that we think can be put to good use. We believe that as you read this book and examine the appendixes, you will understand that it is possible to "crack the code" on creating startups that work.

## Two

To Get Where You're Going, You've Got to Have a Map

Horatio Alger never saw anything like this. The volatile boom-and-bust cycle of recent business history has focused a harsh spotlight on startup ventures, which, among other things, has certainly stripped the romanticized sheen that had come to swathe the entrepreneur's world. The American Dream is alive, but a strong dose of reality has washed back over that entrepreneurial spirit, leaving at the very least some sobering views on how to stalk success. There are lessons amid the casualties, but perhaps more can be learned from the survivors who endured and continued moving forward. In their stories are the case studies that we believe illuminate so well the results of our study.

On January 3, 2000, for example, shares of Akamai Technologies, Inc. reached an inconceivable price of $345 each. For a startup that was not yet two years old, Akamai was among the highest of the high-flyers of the dot-com boom. The previous October, the company had filed what became a blockbuster initial public offering with shares soaring to $145 on its first day. By January, chief executive George Conrades, an industry veteran who had spent twenty-five years at IBM, found himself with a paper fortune of $1.8 billion and more than 300 of the company's 1,300 employees were also paper millionaires.

Akamai, which helped companies do business on the Internet using a vast web of far-flung servers, had been started by a group of very smart technologists from MIT whose goal was to do nothing less than change the way the Internet worked. By putting thousands of servers out in widespread geographic locations and using patented software, Akamai could host Web sites for its customers, which both lowered the cost and ameliorated the logjams that plagued the Internet. Its unique technology had grabbed the attention of the burgeoning dot-com marketplace, and *Akamai*, the Hawaiian word for smart or "cool," became the vendor of choice for the thousands of Internet startups as well as corporate giants seeking to enter the world of e-business on the Web.

When the bubble burst in late 2000, Akamai was hit hard. Legions of its dot-com customers went out of business and the company's stock began to tumble. The tragic events of September 11, 2001 were felt with particular anguish at Akamai when one of its founders and guiding lights, thirty-one-year-old Daniel Lewin, was killed on American Airlines Flight 11, which struck the north tower on that fateful morning. As chief technologist and an immensely popular figure inside of Akamai, Lewin's loss sent the company reeling. Refocusing on business seemed the furthest thing from anyone's mind.

But there was business to be attended to and the economic plunge after 9/11 only made the situation more dire. With a major rethinking about online business, Akamai's *raison d'être* suddenly seemed suspect and Wall Street reacted sharply. Shares began to plunge, and by late 2002 they were trading at 50 cents. Deep cost-cutting resulted in the layoffs of more than half the workforce, and some pundits assumed that Akamai would become yet another casualty of the dot-com bust. Akamai's faithful hung onto the fact that the company was not, in fact, a dot-com but a real startup with proven technology and a vast amount of potential.

Most startup companies endure difficult transitions and understand the perilous nature of survival. It is no surprise that seven out of ten high-tech startups never reach their fifth birthday. For Akamai, the dramatic rollercoaster ride from its founding to its close brush with mortality serves as a microcosm for the early life cycle of a young company. Although few companies have flown so high and plunged so low so quickly, Akamai has not only survived but has begun the arduous climb toward long-term success. By mid-2004, the stock had risen to a respectable $16 per share, and both the fiscal and strategic future of the company looked very solid.

Within Akamai's story and similar stories from any number of startup ventures, one can find important lessons about the quest for success in a startup organization. The reason for Akamai's survival is, on the surface, a simple one: the founders were able to create value in the marketplace. Not unlike Staples, Home Depot, Dell Computer, or Amazon.com, the entrepreneurs and venture capitalists who fashion ideas into actual companies understand that value creation must be at the heart of any enterprise if it is to have a chance of sustainability and growth.

This notion was sidetracked during the Internet bubble of the late 1990s, but it was never truly lost. Our initial research, most of which took place during that very bubble and the immediate aftermath, proves, if nothing else, that the quest for value creation, however one defines it, was never far from the initial business plan. Our subsequent research and case studies indicated results that were the same. To create value you have to follow a plan. The odds of creating a viable company are slim if details are sketchy about how the company actually makes money. And while some companies began to believe that there were shortcuts to the pot of gold, market realities relatively quickly shook people out of their reveries and returned them from Oz. We're back in Kansas now, Toto, and for that, serious entrepreneurs have breathed a huge sigh of relief.

What we realized, as we thought about the structure of our research and the resulting book, was that most of the literature surrounding startup ventures concerns raising finances and selecting companies. Certainly for the venture capital community, historically, the emphasis has been on those two issues. When venture capitalists are looking at a pool of companies trying to raise money in a first or second round of financing, or when preparing to take a company public, most of the metrics that are used are financial. It is akin to looking in a rearview mirror: How much did you spend last year? How much did you make last year? What was your burn rate last year? In truth, while important, that is a limited set of data.

Very little, however, has been written about *managing* these investments, for both the entrepreneurs themselves and the venture capitalists (VCs) who invest in them.

We thought, what if we could find a broader set of metrics that would help focus on the management of a venture once the selection process is over? So many deals that result in failure are due to poor management, especially during the first crucial years in existence. If we could identify metrics that would place value on the capabilities of the management team, the intellectual property, the role of the VC, the role of the board, the competitive marketplace, marketing as a core capability, and a raft of other related issues, we could create diagrams that just might offer a very different but intensely valuable set of lessons. Why not take a closer look at those very management issues and offer up a set of lessons from those who have succeeded?

And that is what we have done. In the emergence from the dotcom meltdown, the current entrepreneurial environment is truly back to the future, and there is more time for thinking about and evaluating the creation of value. After a drought in early-stage financing after the meltdown, there is now a quiet but growing return to seed-stage financing among venture capital firms. According to *BusinessWeek,* investor confidence in early-stage startups is growing again, and as of midyear 2004, fifteen new venture firms have been raising funds over the past two years. After watching seed investments drop from $3 billion in 2000 to less than $400 million in 2003, the VC community is embracing early-stage companies once again.

Talk to any number of veterans of the halcyon days of the Silicon Valley/Route 128 region and you will hear them say that what we are currently experiencing is nothing more than a return to the metrics of the early to mid-1990s, before companies were reaping millions from IPOs based on three PowerPoint slides and a one-page business plan—before people lost sight of what actually creates real, sustainable value.

For example, by creating Star Charts around these metrics, we have been able to identify nine axes upon which to focus attention:

- Market size
- Competitive position
- Business model
- Cash flow
- Investor value contributed
- Strength of the management team
- Product development
- Channel/Alliances
- Customer acquisition

Layered as a foundation element to these nine drivers is marketing and the idea that everyone in a startup must double as a marketer for the company regardless of their official role. We found that this is a common trait of successful startups. Taken alone, none of these drivers of value leap out as examples of unconventional wisdom. Business theorists might assume that most entrepreneurs focus on such a list as they are scribbling their ideas on IHOP napkins at 3 A.M. Yet in truth, the coordinated effort of these nine elements was generally either lost or ignored through the dot-com bubble and has been less intuitive within startups both before and after the bubble than one might assume.

In other words, building successful startup companies is less about that magical eureka moment than it is about doing the hard, focused grunt work in a sustained and coordinated way against these nine sets of processes throughout the early stages of birth and growth.

Akamai's emergence from the brink of the dot-com meltdown, therefore, was less about serendipity than it was about the company's focus on these elements of value creation. Under Conrades— whose impressive industry experience bespeaks an intuitive understanding of all these success factors—Akamai has maintained a disciplined approach on its journey from early-stage startup through survival mode into a new phase of growth. The role of leadership, for example, is often not given enough emphasis. Lip service is paid, but in truth, many startups founder because there is a fundamental disconnect among the founder, the investors, and the early company leaders. A good choice in leadership at the right time can mean the difference between success and failure.

Akamai turned to Conrades, a high-profile industry veteran who had once been in line for the chief executive's job at IBM. Despite Akamai's rollercoaster existence, Conrades has been a crucial influence, a calm hand on the tiller whose willingness to remain with the enterprise throughout its precarious, short existence has played a significant role in its fortunes. Young companies such as Google, which turned to industry veteran Eric Schmidt, former CEO of Novell, and Yahoo!, which brought in Terry Semel, former head of Warner Brothers, in both cases later in the growth cycle, also have forged winning strategies. Why

does one succeed and another fail? In our chapter on management teams and leadership, we will explore these questions and
offer up the wisdom of our research.

It's no surprise that in the course of this research we would ultimately discover that individual startups thrive or fail for reasons often specific to that particular enterprise. One company's
ceiling is another company's floor, no doubt. And yet, we also
found that these nine common metrics, if considered within
the context of your particular venture, will offer much needed
insight.

Conventional wisdom, for example, says that a company first
into its marketplace has a huge advantage in terms of building
market share, brand identification, and credibility. Yet entrepreneur Yuchun Lee, the thirty-eight-year-old founder of Unica Software Corporation, a marketing software maker in Waltham,
Massachusetts, realized quickly that first-mover advantage is
really no advantage at all in the enterprise software space. "My
experience," says Lee, a native of Taiwan and an MIT Sloan
School graduate, "is that the successful companies in high-tech
enterprise software are not the first wave to market but really the
early second wave."

Why? "It's very expensive to educate a market," Lee says.
"When the first wave goes into a market, nobody has heard of this
software category, so they don't know what it does. You have to
spend tremendous energy and resources to educate the market. It
can take years. Even if you are very good at it, it will take at least
a year or two before people understand the value. With the usual
business and budget cycles, it can take three years and you still
have no revenue. So our strategy is to focus on markets that have
already taken shape and go in and compete and beat out the first
wave."

———

EDWARD ROBERTS

David Sarnoff Professor of Management of
Technology, Sloan School of Management, MIT

Q: As a researcher at MIT, you have studied startups for
years. What determines whether they succeed or fail?

Roberts: We did a very detailed quantitative analysis some
years ago that I still think is up to date. In that research we
had several different definitions of success. First, we talked
about survival. Then we talked about success, beyond
simple survival. Then we talked about super success.
These definitions make a difference. If you're just talking
about what does it take to have a company continue on
forever, without really going anyplace, the answer almost
always is that it does not take very much except being
good at something that's technical. It turns out the death
rate for technically based companies is very low.

Because of the skill sets, backgrounds, and the usual
degrees of uniqueness of technical companies, they can
stay in business almost as long as they want unless they
really require huge amounts of capital. For that reason, I
think survival is a lousy metric for success because it
doesn't differentiate.

So then you say, "Okay, what do you mean by reasonable success?" To define reasonable success, we looked at
growth rates, profitability levels, and something I call
"stability of growth and profitability." That means if you
were growing at a rapid pace, but there is high volatility
in your growth, you weren't as good as somebody that
might be growing somewhat more slowly but with a lot of
stability to that growth. And, with respect to profitability,
in my view, slightly higher profitability—but with higher

volatility—is less desirable than a slightly lower level of profitability but with more stability. So we tended to look both at profitability and growth as our success measures.

When we did that, what we found was that our sample of 850 startups clustered into several groups. About 50 percent of the 850 companies we studied were what we called mere survivors. They didn't go very far at all, but they didn't fail either. Another 15 percent of the companies we studied went out of business pretty quickly. They just didn't make it. And then you basically have one third of our sample of companies left. This last group could be divided almost fifty/fifty between those that were reasonably successful and those that were very successful.

Q: What differentiates relatively successful companies from super successful companies?

Roberts: We found relatively few things that were strong differentiators with regard to levels of success. Even so, one thing did show up that I think is a really important thing. What showed up was that individual entrepreneurs *don't* succeed, teams *do* succeed.

Q: Please explain what you mean.

Roberts: We found very strong data that said that the larger the size of the founding group, the greater the likelihood that the team and the company would succeed. A company's chances for success went up dramatically from a solo-founded company to a two-founder company to a three-founder company to a four-founder company. As you went from one, to two, to three, to four founders, you had dramatic upward changes in the probability of success. These changes were statistically significant.

Q: What did you attribute that to?

Roberts: The first thing is the larger the founder group, the greater its diversity of skill sets. Larger groups tended to have someone with marketing skills. Marketing was far less likely to be one of the skills represented in a solo entrepreneur. So the more people starting a company, the more skill sets the company has to draw upon.

The second thing that came up was that with larger groups you had larger amounts of initial capital. The reason for that is that initial capital tends to be contributed capital, so more founders, more capital contributed by the founders, their friends, and their families.

With more initial capital, there is an increased likelihood that the company would focus on products, not just on generating revenue. A lot of companies get started, and they find themselves in a revenue bind and they do things to raise money just to keep going. They sell services, they create custom products, they do things that couldn't possibly be where they want to end up because those things seem like they are pathways to revenue.

There's another element here, too. When you start with a solo founder, you have to build a team during the life of the company. Then, when you do it, you are often building a team of people who haven't worked together before. But when you start with a cluster of cofounders, that cluster usually comes out of a single work environment where they had prior work relationships. They knew each other's strengths and weaknesses. In addition, there was a leader to the group. The leader usually becomes the CEO of the startup and is accepted by the other people who are cofounders because they've worked together before. So, there are a number of dimensions relating to size that contributes to a company's chances of success.

Q: Did you find any other contributors to success?

Roberts: Companies that had a marketing or salesperson at the beginning did better than those that did not. Having a marketing or salesperson as a cofounder seems to be critical.

Q: There is a point of view that says that people working in startups should view themselves as marketers, no matter what they do. Do you agree with that?

Roberts: Not really. Technical people who are really technical people usually have a high degree of skepticism about marketing people. So I think you need to have marketing independently represented within the founding group and company. Marketing people have to have their own seat at the table. But not everybody has to sit in the seat. It's okay for the technical lead guy to fight with the marketing lead guy. It's fine because it's just one of the ongoing conflicts that exists. We didn't find that everybody in the company needed to be market oriented. But what we have asserted is that a company needs to have a marketing orientation.

Q: Are there any common traits of successful entrepreneurs?

Roberts: First, I would say the focus. I did some studies and found that entrepreneurs are people with high needs for achievement personally. Entrepreneurs have moderate needs for power, and they are people for whom affiliation doesn't matter at all. We ended up finding that the strong need for achievement was really a need to be independent, to do things on your own, and to create stuff that manifests itself tangibly. Entrepreneurs really like accomplishments that are visible—like buildings or money or something or other like that. Building an organization that has some size, that's a meaningful achievement to them. In addition, entrepreneurs want to contribute. They didn't want to just "luck into it." So if you won a crap shoot or you won the lottery and got $10 million, entrepreneurs would not regard it as having achieved something. In addition, we actually found that a moderate need for power was much better than a high need for power and much better than a low need for power. If you had a low need for power, you left things to everybody's discretion and you didn't create any degree of centralized control while wanting to control everything wasn't good either. So, in the end, what turned out to be critical was that entrepreneurs have a high drive to achieve and also a willingness to share power across at least a group of players.

Q: Have you observed changes in the world of startups over the last few years, in the aftermath of the bubble?

Roberts: What happened with the bubble is that the whole world got changed, and the bursting of the bubble then created a very long recovery period. And I think the fundamental change that occurred was the recovery period. You suddenly had a very different environment for getting funded. It was not just that the VCs went back to first principles of what they thought and what they believed in. It's also that they became terribly gun shy.

As a result, you have an interesting problem. A large numbers of venture capitalists have their funds expiring in the next year or so based on when they raised the money. And they haven't committed their money because they're sitting with deep pockets but are gun shy and afraid to invest. And you have some degree of shift taking place right now, sort of a rush to market. So we have a bunch of panicking VCs who are saying, "Damn it, I'm never going to get this money invested. And if I have to go back to my investors and ask for more time, they'll say screw you, you've done nothing for me for all these years. Give me back my money at no carry and no charges." So a lot of guys are trying to unload their money right now, in 2004.

But if you go back a year ago, and the prior two years to the 2002 and 2003 time period, once the bubble crashed, you had a period of time when it was extraordinarily dif-

ficult for an entrepreneur to raise money. This included
angel money. Angels were scared away, too. Angels didn't
invest because they wondered, "Is there ever going to be a
time when I'm going to be able to liquidate my investment?" So terrible things happened. I think the mood is
changing now.

There's another substantive change that I've observed
over the last ten years. Intellectual property is taking on a
much stronger role than it used to. Intellectual property,
even in high-tech stuff, by and large was unimportant. It
was important in biology and biotechnology, but it wasn't
important in anything else. Now it's really important in
biotechnology, but suddenly it's also really important in a
whole bunch of other areas. Existing companies, startups,
and VCs are worrying whether anything they own—their
intellectual property—is going to stand the test of a court
fight. That's different.

Conventional wisdom, again, went by the wayside with the
advent of the Internet as a burgeoning business venue. Our research showed that the most successful software companies paid
more attention than their less successful counterparts to growing
revenue and to building a scalable business model. These companies also made greater and steadier progress on the product development value axis.

Jeff Taylor, for example, embodies the Internet entrepreneur.
While running a small, avant-garde advertising agency in Boston
in the mid-1990s, Taylor heard a client say, "We don't want great
ideas. We want a monster idea." Not long afterward, Taylor
awoke at 4:30 A.M. from a dream about a giant jobs posting bulletin board that he would call The Monster Board. Even before the
term World Wide Web became a part of the global lexicon, Taylor
envisioned a digital site where prospective job seekers and hirers
could go to find each other. He sketched out his plan on a napkin

in a coffee shop and gathered a team within his agency to develop the product into reality.

He focused on building a scalable business model. He married the past and the future in elegant harmony. The concept of job postings hadn't changed in five hundred years, when someone would nail a note to a tree or doorway looking for an employee with a certain skill. The typical resume also hadn't changed dramatically in one hundred years, Taylor says. But by offering an online site where job seekers and employers could connect directly, Taylor managed to disintermediate the newspaper Help Wanted section.

Within that model, he incorporated partnerships and critical channel alliances with giant media outlets like *USA Today* and Ziff-Davis. Early on, The Monster Board was simply a hot link from the Web sites of these partners. Soon, however, Taylor saw that most of the traffic was coming directly to Monster.com, and he decided to focus his efforts and resources there.

In a bold stroke, atypical of most technology startups, Taylor decided to spend more than $3 million to buy three thirty-second advertising spots during the 1999 Super Bowl broadcast. The award-winning black and white ads, entitled "When I Grow Up," featured children musing on their future careers. The response was overwhelming and not only fueled massive growth for the Web-based business but catapulted Monster to brand status among Web sites.

Taylor points out that while the Super Bowl ads were a bold if risky stroke, the key was that his business model had been carefully conceived and executed so that the nascent company could handle the outpouring of interest. "One of my experiences watching companies fall apart all around me was that if you don't have a good business model, you can't make up a business model," Taylor says. "With no business model, an ad during the Super Bowl doesn't do anything except get you in hot water faster."

Other startups tried advertising during the Super Bowl amid the Internet bubble. It's a good bet that only trivia buffs can remember their names today. Why Taylor's model worked while others failed is open to debate. Yet there is no contesting the fact that when one examines the evolution of Monster.com, one discovers a blend of out-of-the-box thinking coupled with a disciplined attention to the metrics we have laid out above.

Early-stage companies, by their very nature, are a study in chaos theory. Every day is a sixteen-hour sprint for survival, and the very adrenaline that fuels the commitment of the core team and its employees leaves countless opportunities for eyes to be distracted from the core business metrics. In truth, the environment at early-stage companies is extremely confusing. There is very little structure and, thus, there is great difficulty in establishing forward momentum.

Establishing a framework from the outset, such as how the initial investment should be allocated and targeted, tends to shift on an as-needed basis. Entrepreneurs find themselves tugged and pulled in many directions simultaneously. They compose lists of target goals:

- With my first money, I should accomplish the following things . . .

- I may not need customers immediately, but I do need to establish our intellectual property.

- I need the beginnings of a management team.

- I need to find industry focus or some kind of industry engagement.

- I need to create some level of product development so that we can demonstrate the technology and speculate on a product mix.

But often enough, the balance shifts and attention is diverted. Rather than a tree growing out symmetrically in concentric rings, growth occurs in one place to the detriment of a separate but crucial other need. For example, it may seem intuitive to get to the market quickly and sign up customers immediately, but if the intellectual property is not in place, the early customer relationships can be meaningless. Failure lurks around the corner.

The power of the Star Charts that our research spawned is that they help establish baselines for companies in a variety of technology sectors, including software, semiconductors, telecommunications, services, and Internet-based startups. By establishing the metrics that our research revealed as the key components of a framework for early-stage companies, entrepreneurs can accomplish two key things: focus and synchronicity. Effective leaders have laser focus on their vision and the ability to shift and revisit and rethink the path to get there. They also understand that the early stage of a company's existence is a strange and sometimes bizarre dance. Synchronizing the efforts, finding the balance, connecting all the pieces of the spiral are at the heart of why startups succeed.

As we look more closely at the metrics of our research in the following chapters, our goal is to offer up a framework with which to achieve such focus and synchronicity. We will emphasize the importance of leadership from the management team and investors and the organic, natural growth phases that define the basis of a new company's development.

## Three

Management: Nothing Ever Happens Without Great People

Ask any investor or industry participant why startup companies succeed and the universal answer is "because of the management team." The conventional wisdom among technology industry veterans is that great companies are built by great teams. A strong, experienced, multiskilled team will find a way to turn an average idea into a winner, but an average team will kill a great idea every time.

Talk to any knowledgeable venture veteran or entrepreneur and they will likely tell you that the management team is the number one measurement when predicting success of a new company. In fact, most VCs will focus intensely on the team and walk away from a deal, regardless of how exciting the idea or technology might be, if they don't rate the team highly.

John Doerr, the legendary partner at Kleiner, Perkins, Caufield & Byers, the celebrated Silicon Valley venture firm, told *Fast Company* magazine, "In the world today, there's plenty of technology, plenty of entrepreneurs, plenty of money, plenty of venture capital. What's in short supply is great teams. Your biggest challenge will be building a great team. There's enormous change under way in every facet of the world. Some is technology driven, some is market driven. All that change creates unprecedented opportunity. But to take full advantage of those opportunities, focus on the team. Teams win."

Certainly the money flows to the strongest teams, and success generally follows the money. This is true not just in venture-funded high-tech industries but also in the more mundane realms of business as well. The first rule for business might as well be, "It's the people, stupid." That's the conventional wisdom.

Yet our research and our discussions with entrepreneurs, professional managers, and venture capitalists uncovered more than a few unconventional wrinkles within the conventional wisdom. In relation to financing, for example, the experience and completeness of a company's management team had a positive impact on success in later rounds of financing. But we also found that fielding a high-powered management team at the seed stages did not necessarily provide an advantage. In fact, creating a top-heavy organization too early in a company's development burns up too much cash, may leave the company without needed resources to do the work, and demands more infrastructure, which can end up disrupting the focus needed at the outset. Thus, creating a perfectly balanced team in the seed stage or early rounds is a nuanced but essential task.

———

MARK J. LEVIN

Chairman, President, CEO,
Millennium Pharmaceuticals

Q: How do you measure success?

Levin: First, we're talking about Millennium, which is a pharmaceutical company, so the first criteria of success is making a big difference in patients' lives. That's why we started the company in the first place, and that's what all of our ongoing efforts are about.

But in addition, we're also talking about creating significant shareholder return, and not just for one year. What we are talking about is creating shareholder return that is continuous and long term. We are talking about creating something that is a big success for the investor. After that, success is creating something big for the people that come into the company. That includes creating an environment where someone can build a successful career in a great place to work. It includes creating an environment that allows people to do great things. So when we talk about success, we are really talking about something that is multidimensional—success for patients, investors, and the people who work here, over the long term.

Q: How do you achieve success?

Levin: When we started the company, we determined that the key to success was our people. We had to have the right people. I worked for a guy in venture capital named Tommy Davis, who was one of the founders of the whole venture capital industry. He started in the '50s in venture capital and was one of the most successful people in that field.

And when I joined the Mayfield Fund in the late '80s, Tommy had Parkinson's and was getting ready to retire. But I had a chance to talk to him a couple times. The point he would make was that while thousands of people came to Mayfield over the years looking for an investment, he would only invest in what he called a "fantastic team." Why? Because, he said, a fantastic team will take the average idea and turn it into something great. But he also said that an average team can take a fantastic idea and be unsuccessful with it.

This is clearly true in venture capital and it is clearly true here. Millennium was based on bringing together an unusual group of outstanding people, starting with the four founders, who were academics and who led the largest genome center in the world. They had unbelievable scientific capabilities and accomplishments. They had a real vision about the future of genomics and what it would do. Then, when it came to investors, we involved the cream of the crop. Venrock, Kleiner Perkins, Mayfield, Greylock. This initial group fit Tommy Davis's definition of a "fantastic team."

We then hired some incredible people. In fact, we hired some brilliant people early on, great science people, great businesspeople. So, during our initial couple years, our aim was to bring together a great team of people in all aspects. I think that was absolutely key to what we did. And it's key to what we do now—create fantastic teams.

Q: How do you build a team and not just a group of individuals?

Levin: That's an important point. One of the things that is key is that you can't just have great people; they have to work together. They have to form a team. And just like any other startup, we had our adventures. Some of the people just didn't get along. It was personalities, and we had a lot of interesting personalities. One of the interesting dynamics that was happening at the time was geneticists or *genomicists* were—for the first time—getting attention from the world. As a result, they were evolving into superstars of science. Everyone was paying attention to them.

Because they got more attention probably than any group, every venture capital firm was fawning over them. They were really in demand. But at the end of the day, people realized how important it was that they stay together. At the end of the day, they realized they could really do something special together. They understood that it was much easier to do it together, as a team, than to try to do it alone, as individuals.

Q: How did you get them to understand the importance of building a fantastic team?

Levin: It took a driving vision. It took spending a lot of time with people and building them into a team. It took concentrating on team building early. It took making everyone understand it was key to our success. That's key for the long term.

Let me reiterate. To me the most important ingredient of long-term success is hiring great people, building a culture where great people can do great things. And then to let them do it. Empower them, hold them accountable—obviously—but give them a clear vision and strategy and work with them on developing their goals for the future. At the end of the day, you have to have great people to make something fantastic happen.

In truth, the technology sector, even after the dot-com meltdown and the advent of the new millennium, is still a maelstrom of conflicting philosophies and turf battles between the technologists and those who seek to carry their ideas to financially rewarding conclusions. Entrepreneurs, by their very nature, are self-starters with strong egos and even stronger opinions about how they plan to change the world. They tend to believe deeply in their ideas and are often intractable about listening to objective opinions. Finding the perfect blend of an effective management team is difficult enough. But finding an entrepreneur with enough self-awareness to readily cede power and authority at the earliest stages of a new venture can be daunting.

"Most startups start with an entrepreneur's dream, a passionate evocation of a solution dying to be born," Rohit Shukla, CEO of the Los Angeles Regional Technology Alliance, told *Business-Week* in 2002. "But in a business environment where information flies around unencumbered by previous bounds of convention or technology, it is very likely that many people have approached a specific problem with solutions that, while they are not identical, are similar enough and plausible enough to complicate even the most vivid dream. Yet many startup entrepreneurs, jealous of their dream, refuse to part with it, and risk being the big fish in a shrinking pond instead of sharing their dream with a team who can shape and guide it into open water."

KEY CHARACTERISTICS

Gauging the strength of a management team is more art than science. Our research illustrates the importance of management teams in virtually every technology sector, and our cases found that there are several key characteristics:

- Venture capitalists talk about people, people, and people. They will always bet on fantastic teams over fantastic products.

- Winning teams identify the leader at the outset. Partnerships in which this is unclear tend to fail or run into problems.

- Yet the *wrong* CEO, even one with the right idea, will sink a startup.

- Founding *teams* with a diverse set of skills tend to be far more successful than a single founding entrepreneur, especially if the members of the team worked together previously and had complementary skills and personalities.

- Knowing when to bring in professional management to a new venture is difficult but crucial. Professional management, force-fed into a new venture too early, will undoubtedly create friction and alienate the founding entrepreneurs whose passion and vision are crucial.

- Being smart is a commodity, table stakes to the game. So, successful technology entrepreneurs, along with a strong vision, ability to lead, and charisma, must also have discipline, focus, the ability to adapt and learn, as well as a keen sense of listening. Given that these traits tend to be diametrically opposed, the potential for success tends to rest with the outside investors' skill at integrating professional management into a new venture.

- Among the hardest skills to find are leaders who deeply understand the marketplace and how to competitively position themselves in that marketplace.

THE ENTREPRENEURS

John Landry, chairman and chief technology officer at Adesso Systems, a Boston-based wireless applications software startup, has either started, invested in, or been on the boards of a dozen technology startups during his lengthy career. He also served in executive positions at IBM and Lotus Development Corporation. Landry believes deeply, from firsthand experience, that an entrepreneur cannot hope to build a successful company by himself. The optimum scenario, Landry believes, is for an entrepreneur to find someone or several people with complementary skills. If the entrepreneur is a technologist, for example, he or she must seek out a chief executive with sales, marketing, and operational skills.

Yet Landry is constantly surprised at the number of entrepreneurs who don't understand or are unwilling to embrace the importance of the team and continue to insist on doing it alone. In a recent encounter with a software company on whose board Landry sits, the founder, who had worked only in large companies, insisted that he should assume the CEO role despite his lack of experience in small startup ventures. As the technology vision-ary, the founder should have been the chief technology officer and looked to a savvy operations veteran to become CEO. But in this case, the founder insisted on running the show. "Things went wrong," Landry says. "Not enough attention was being paid to the technology because he was busy being CEO. There was no CTO, and as a result, the company missed a key product intro-duction."

While the obstinate entrepreneur issue is easier to address and resolve in venture-backed startups—i.e., the VCs have enough in-fluence on the board to insist on a change in the management team—it is a tougher problem in startups that were bootstrapped or backed by angel investors.

Landry understands that it is challenging to force relationships on entrepreneurs. In many instances, where lead investors insist on placing professional management into an entrepreneur's startup, trouble emerges. "It is much harder for the founder to ad-just to a new CEO of the company that he founded," Landry says. "At the end of the day, personalities and emotion play a huge role, particularly at the top."

The quest for a strong team in a startup venture often relies on little more than gut feel and intuition. Jamie Rapperport, founder and executive vice president of Vendavo, a leading provider of price management software based in Palo Alto, California, has a twenty-year technology track record, working with several suc-cessful startup ventures. "Part of what you are doing as an entre-preneur is getting together a collection of people who you feel you can work with," Rapperport says. "And to some extent, the test of whether or not you feel you can work with them is going to be a proxy for whether they can work with one another." The team, therefore, will directly reflect the personality of the entre-preneur, for better or worse, and set the tone for the culture of the new enterprise.

More often than not, a strong management team is an accurate barometer for future success. But can it backfire? Can too much focus be placed on the management team at the wrong time in a startup's evolution? For example, some startups can fall into the same trap as Webvan, a highly visible casualty of the dot-com boom, which placed too much emphasis on the team at the wrong stage of its growth.

By bringing in a high-powered, highly compensated management team, including former Accenture CEO, George Shaheen, Webvan, an online grocery delivery startup, got ahead of itself. The nascent company hadn't taken the time to prototype its concept, test it with customers, validate the market and the value proposition. Instead, it poured vital resources into procuring a high-powered, highly visible management team, and the result was disastrous. A promising concept got sidetracked and eventually failed. So, a high-level management team with great ambition turns out to not be value neutral: it can be value negative.

"The most important thing is having a product," Landry states. "If you bring in the team before you have a product, the team has nothing to do."

In fact, he points out, a management team, fueled by impatience and anxious to become a real company, may create an unrealistic "pull" on the product, often coercing the developers to ship products prematurely. "I've seen this many times," Landry says. "The team says, 'We've been here six months. We thought the product was supposed to be done.' So they ship it and it doesn't work. The customer sends it back, the sales guys are all pissed off, and all of a sudden there is endless friction because you've built the team before the product was ready."

TIMING IS EVERYTHING

Timing the creation of the management team, therefore, is a more finely tuned experience than meets the eye. At Adesso Systems, for example, the company was actually little more than a development shop for its first two years. Landry didn't hire anyone, including Dennis Kelly, the current CEO, until the product was robust and ready to be sold. "That's the time to build the team," Landry states.

Yuchun Lee, the CEO of Unica Software, founded his company in 1992 with a different point of view. Though Lee, who was then working at Digital Equipment Corporation, knew he wanted to build a software product company, he believed that he needed a strong, complementary team from the outset. His two cofounders, Ruby Kennedy and David Cheung, both data mining experts and skilled technologists, still remain key contributors to Unica today.

Lee, who bootstrapped his venture, is a disciple of Edward B. Roberts, a professor of the management of technology at MIT's Sloan School of Management, whose 1991 book *Entrepreneurs in High Technology* measured the profitability and growth of technology startups. Lee, a Sloan School graduate, agrees with Roberts' finding: individual entrepreneurs don't succeed, teams succeed. In fact, Roberts, who chairs the MIT Entrepreneurship Center, found that the larger the size of the founding group, the greater the likelihood that the company will succeed.

Among the reasons, Roberts says, is that larger groups tended to have a greater diversity of skill sets and a greater likelihood that essential marketing and sales expertise was included at the outset.

Unica, which makes enterprise marketing software, remains privately held, and Lee has a clear-sighted goal to grow the company into a $1 billion software giant. He praises his management team and board as "extremely talented" and acknowledges that any CEO of a startup, including himself, may not be able to handle such growth. But he is unusual as an entrepreneur in that he is a student of business first, a technologist second.

"I actually enjoy the building process of a company," he says. "I read a lot of business books and continue to exercise these new muscles. Even though I haven't run a company as big as Unica is today, I think I'm always staying a few steps in front of it."

Lee insists that Unica's culture is built upon "brutal honesty," and if he were no longer doing his job, if the company was scaling beyond his ability, he'd be told immediately and he would step away. Our research showed that most entrepreneurs are less self-effacing about this thorny issue.

THE VENTURE CAPITALISTS

Alex Osadzinski, forty-eight, is a partner at Trinity Ventures, a venture capital firm on the renowned Sand Hill Road in Menlo Park, California, in the heart of Silicon Valley. Osadzinski spent most of his career working at startups in various phases of development. He ran European marketing for five years for Sun Microsystems shortly after it was founded in the early 1980s and before it became a public company. He has been part of a diverse group of management teams and has heard most of the war stories.

The founder/CEO who is holding back his or her startup is a known type among savvy venture investors. Before making an investment, venture backers always ask an entrepreneur, "What are your plans?" The answer, Osadzinski says, is always the same. "Here's what they will tell you: 'I want the company to be successful. For the right person, I will step aside in an instant, but I think I can take the company quite a way. Of course, I want what's best for the company.' But here's how to read between the lines. What they are really saying is: 'You'll have to pry my cold, dead hands off the steering wheel!'"

As our research showed, the role of the leader shifts significantly at different stages of the business. During the early stage, when the CEO is concentrating on product development, building a prototype, adding members to the team, and scoping out the marketplace and competition, the demands on the leader are quite different than in later stages of company evolution. A company that has survived its seed and early round stages and heads into the build-out of the product, the advent of the sales and marketing function, and the creation of a brand within its marketplace will need a dramatically different type of leader. Most entrepreneurs are not wired to make such dynamic changes in their style and strategic thinking. Often it is a different person who needs to take the lead position, and the VCs tend to be the first to note this sea change in the company.

Osadzinski, who grew up in England, the child of Polish immigrant parents, joined his first startup at the age of twenty in the United Kingdom. Entrepreneurs, he says, must be "driven, focused, and very confident, because it's easy to point to the hundreds of reasons a startup will fail." Thus, entrepreneurs tend to be the worst judge of their own management capabilities and longevity, leaving it to the investors to bring a time-tested "pattern recognition" for what he calls "investable CEOs."

"Investable means he or she will take the startup as far as they can and will step aside and help bring in someone else" to run the venture, Osadzinski explains. "Investors know if the CEO needs to be replaced in due course. It always takes longer than you want. But if it's the wrong CEO, that CEO will drive the company out of business."

Though some venture capitalists say, "Give me big markets and I'll find a good management team," most veteran VCs put most of their emphasis on identifying great entrepreneurial teams. Wade Woodson, a senior partner with Sigma Partners in Menlo Park, California, says, "For people who talk about looking for great markets, I ask, who finds them those great markets? The answer is the great entrepreneurs who lead them there."

THE PROFESSIONAL MANAGERS

Among the most heinous of the Internet bubble's transgressions was the creation of false and misleading indicators of value. Management teams envisioned short-term exit strategies, usually quick, hot IPOs that would reap hundreds of millions of dollars for founders and investors.

In normal markets, while most entrepreneurs define success as taking a startup from inception to a lucrative initial public offering, the reality is that most technology startups with real value end up as acquisition candidates rather than as public companies.

Cisco Systems, the networking giant based in San Jose, California, has acquired dozens of startups since the early 1990s in order to build its product and customer base. Its primary criterion in judging value is the strength of the management team.

Charles Giancarlo, Cisco's senior vice president and general manager of product development, has been instrumental in many of those acquisitions over the years. Giancarlo himself arrived at Cisco in 1994 as part of the acquisition of Kalpana, an Ethernet switching startup that Giancarlo helped rescue from early management troubles.

Cisco has developed a strategy for acquisition intended to minimize the number of bad choices. Cisco seeks to fill holes in its technology offerings or simply watches for promising new technology to add to its arsenal. But a strong management team is a prerequisite for acquisition. "If the management team is really good, you would expect the technology piece to be pretty good, too," Giancarlo says.

But the strength of the management team is key simply because Cisco focuses not just on the acquisition but also on the integration of the company into Cisco's culture and product mix. A key requirement is to keep most or all of the management team in place so that particular team can realize the promise of its technology dream. In order to get a return on an acquisition investment, Cisco must extrapolate what sales of the product will be years into the future, so it is betting heavily on the team that it acquires to produce results.

"Before we make an acquisition, we look at what motivates the management team," Giancarlo says. "If what motivates them is money, then it's probably not the right team to buy."

What Cisco seeks are people who are not simply interested in financial reward or running their own show but want to see their ideas become reality and their products built, adopted, and utilized in the real world.

"We want people who want to change the world," Giancarlo says. "Because by coming in and being part of Cisco, they have a vehicle by which they can get the thing they've built into the hands of a lot of customers. They can beat the competition and make the fruits of their labor very successful."

In fact, much of the preacquisition discussion focuses on this very aspect of the management team, and Cisco has walked away from many deals in which it believed the management team was primarily focused on money or wanting to do its own thing.

The introduction of professional management into startups remains a daunting issue for both venture capitalists and technology companies seeking acquisitions. When venture firms can lure veteran leaders to startups, the payoff can be dramatic. For example, a former Cisco executive named Don LeBeau became CEO of Aruba Wireless Networks at the behest of its lead investor Sequoia Capital. LeBeau had been senior vice president of sales and marketing at Cisco from 1992 to 1997 and is credited with driving revenues there from $350 million to $6 billion. LeBeau was lured out of semiretirement in 2004 to replace Aruba's founding CEO, Pankaj Manglik, amid expectations that LeBeau's experience and reputation will take the startup to the next level of success, whether that is closer to an IPO or an acquisition by a company like Cisco.

Another example is Akamai, which also has the advantage of having a veteran chief executive with more than forty years' experience in the technology sector. George Conrades, sixty-five, is both cerebral and passionate about what he is doing and what he hopes to achieve. He would certainly qualify as a "Level 5

Leader," according to Jim Collin's *Good to Great*, disinterested in the personal spotlight but strong-willed and effective. Although he is no longer a billionaire, the Harley-riding CEO has more than enough money to retire comfortably. Yet he can't imagine leaving anytime soon.

"My reason to stay is that this is personal," he states. "It's very important that this company becomes successful. We are fulfilling a mission to create something of value—something valued in the marketplace by customers who say that it helps them. That's what turns everybody on: you are creating value and you are doing it in an unusual way."

Conrades's journey to Akamai did not follow industry convention. As a senior vice president at IBM in the late 1980s, Conrades was on a very short list of candidates to succeed retiring CEO John Akers, when political infighting undermined his long career at Big Blue. He reemerged in 1994 as CEO of BBN, a pioneering software vendor in Cambridge, Massachusetts, and eventually orchestrated the sale of that company to GTE. Unwilling to take his money and retire to the blue highways on his Harley, Conrades began to dabble in venture capital and signed on with a nascent Boston firm named Polaris Ventures. He had hardly hung a picture on his office wall when he met Tom Leighton, a respected MIT professor, and Danny Lewin, one of Leighton's graduate students, who proposed their intriguing concept.

"I knew a good idea when I saw it," Conrades says. "I got very excited about it and Polaris decided to invest. They told me, 'You like this so much, why don't you join the board?' I went one step further and became the CEO."

Not a traditional entrepreneur, Conrades came in as a professional manager with startup fire. When he joined Akamai, Conrades put $2 million of his own money into the venture. His investment was not in stock options but in real cash. The other senior managers put their own money in as well. "The senior management here has an iron will mostly because we own our stock," Conrades says.

FOCUSING ON POSITIVE ATTRIBUTES

Akamai struggled during the recession, but Conrades managed to staunch the bleeding in 2003 and put the company on track to profitability by 2004. In order to turn things around, Conrades focused on the positive attributes that had been a key part of the founding concept and that had survived the turbulence that followed. Akamai is on its way to success for many reasons, but among the most crucial, according to Conrades, are these four:

- Akamai had a big idea—putting computers out at the edge of the Internet to help companies do their Web processing—and that idea did and still does have credibility.

- The technology works. With six million lines of code, Akamai's offerings are complex but reliable and robust. Customers can trust the technology to support their businesses without crashing.

- Despite its rocky ride and a series of painful layoffs, Akamai retained a core group of very talented people. The brainpower is intensely high, and as Conrades has learned, "smart people love smart people," so they are drawn to working in this action-oriented environment.

- No matter how bad things got, Akamai didn't change its mission. While competitors tried jumping from one business to another during the downturn, Akamai stayed the course and it has paid off. The company now carries 15 percent of all Web traffic on a given day.

While Conrades's list is accurate, Akamai's metamorphosis from mere survivor to player with the goal line in sight represents far more than a big idea and an eye on the mission. Under Conrades, Akamai is moving along a path to value built upon a growing set of metrics that provide focus, discipline, and strategic business vision. Most early-stage startups struggle to embrace these metrics, and the usual result is failure. And though awareness of the need for such focus and discipline often gets paid lip service, the reality is that most startups, especially in their earliest days, find themselves in a scattershot environment of crisis management, cash flow conundrums, and management vacuums. This is where leadership and a strong management team can mean the difference between success and failure.

As a young company, Akamai has crammed an entire corporate life cycle into its first five years. The boom-and-bust cycle had taken its toll, and Conrades understood that the time had come to get very businesslike and start making "intelligent decisions about where to spend the money and how." Startups routinely burn through seed money and early venture funding. Akamai was well on its way to burning through even the cash raised during its IPO. It was time for fiscal discipline.

The company had been on a feeding frenzy of massive overhead: hiring hundreds of young workers and leasing exorbitant downtown office space. As the bubble was bursting, Conrades began to come to terms with some stark realities. "We finally had to put in financial metrics, like creating budgets," Conrades says. "We just kept growing up and growing up and kept communicating all the time. It's always better against the backdrop of an emergency so there's a reason and everybody understands and goes along with it."

Perhaps most important for a startup is the makeup of the board of directors, which Conrades began to reshape by replacing venture capitalists and angel investors with professional board members who would bring new and crucial business acumen to the mix.

As we explore the importance of resources as metrics for startup success, we believe the role of the board, which would fall under the heading of management team, is a critical area of focus. As we will see in the next chapter, the role of boards, especially in startup companies, has shifted dramatically from a watchdog role into one of active leadership and strategic guidance.

Four

It's Okay to Be a Watchdog, but Boards Must Create Value

Our research revealed that private equity investors play a far more important role in the success of startups than simply providing funding. After the strength of the management team, the value provided by investors ranked second among resource metrics on the three axes. In addition, a significant number of investors, whether they are venture capitalists or angel investors, retain seats on the boards of startups, giving them not only increased influence but deeper commitment to the future of the new enterprise. Our research suggests that we are in the midst of a dramatic change in both the function and makeup of boards. We expect active, involved boards to play an increasing role in the success of startups.

BEYOND THE WATCHDOG

Since the Internet bubble burst and the recession washed over the technology sector like a tidal wave, startup boards are moving beyond traditional watchdog roles in both subtle and more overt ways. A new generation of professional directors, some retired or semiretired and thus having more time to devote to their directorial duties, are becoming intensely involved in helping to not only create fiscal discipline and focus but also in setting strategic direction.

Startup companies such as Akamai experience distinct growth phases that require different kinds of management experience and involvement as they evolve. As Akamai struggled to find financial stability, for example, it was the company's board of directors that played a key part in putting fiscal processes and controls in place, even insisting that the struggling company keep a minimum cash balance of $100 million on hand at all times. While some entrepreneurs might chafe at such direct input from outside board members, the days of passive boards and silent investors have passed.

Our research confirmed that investors have a strong impact on value creation. While most startups in the research received the bulk of their initial round of financing from venture capital firms, others turned to angels, corporate VCs, corporate investors, management-founders, and incubators. Most of our sample had looked to either VC firms or angel investors for their lead investments. Our research revealed that:

- VCs were more likely to provide strategic assistance than were other types of lead investors.

- Angel investors were more likely than VC firms to provide customer introductions and help in forming strategic alliances.

- As we expected, startups experienced more hands-on assistance from VC firms in the later rounds of financing, which is not surprising for full-time professional investors.

- We also found that by the B round, angel-backed companies seem to have progressed farther than VC-backed startups on all strategy axes, including market size, competitive position, and business model. They tended to be more focused on cash flow management and revenue while VC-backed companies had slightly better management teams at the same stage.

Successful startups tend to rely heavily on investors for advice, wisdom, customer contacts, financial insight, and support during the dark days of doubt and uncertainty that every startup experiences. Venture investors grab board seats in the seed and early rounds of financing, but often wear out their welcome when a startup evolves from seed to survival stage and beyond.

THE IMPACT OF SARBANES-OXLEY

How long venture capitalists should remain on boards is a crucial question for a startup. No clear formula for success has emerged. Some CEOs rely on the VCs for years after the formation of the company, while others itch to replace the VCs as quickly as possible. With VCs often focused on quick exit strategies, they can often create friction about management strategies with entrepreneurs who are looking longer term for their rewards.

With the advent of new securities regulations, such as the Sarbanes-Oxley Act of 2002, boards find themselves in the legal line of fire in ways heretofore unheard of, and they are taking it seriously. Sarbanes-Oxley imposed new criminal penalties for corporate wrongdoing, transformed the way the accounting sector is regulated, and made corporate executives more accountable for the veracity of their financial reports. In other words, it put the fear of God and the SEC into those in charge of corporate governance—and that includes directors.

While some executives and directors curse Sarbanes-Oxley, especially Section 404, for creating mountains of time-plundering paperwork, others see it as a blessing for startup companies. In fact, a growing number of privately held companies are rushing to incorporate Sarbanes-Oxley controls even though they don't have to, according to a July 2004, article in the *New York Times*. By embracing stronger accounting procedures and corporate governance discipline, these companies become more attractive both to venture capitalists looking to invest and to other companies seeking acquisitions. The idea of being private but acting public makes sense to those in the high-technology sector.

Entrepreneurs such as Yuchun Lee of Unica Software illustrate the trend. The board of his still private, still independent software firm is made up of both venture capitalists and outside directors. "The most important thing the board does is force you to run like a public company," Lee says. "I think of it as adult supervision. They don't get involved in day-to-day decision making, but they ask the tough questions, which is really what they are there for."

Martin Coyne, the lead director at Akamai, notes that startups, no matter how strong the management team, don't focus enough on process. "What Sarbanes-Oxley forces a startup to do is realize, if you want to play and you want to adhere to the rules, you need to have processes in place to run your business effectively," Coyne says. "In a way, it provides a beautiful structure that the board can then use to make sure the processes are in place."

Coyne says that when he joined the Akamai board, the new regulations drove him to really pay attention to audits and revenue recognition. "I'll be damned if I'm going to see my name on the front page of the *Wall Street Journal*," Coyne says. So while finding high-quality directors has become tougher, those who do commit to the role are doing so with purpose.

———

JAMIE RAPPERPORT

Founder and former CEO, Executive Vice President
Business Development, Vendavo

Q: You are a veteran entrepreneur. Most recently, you started
Vendavo, which develops pricing software for companies.
What traits do entrepreneurs need to succeed?

Rapperport: Since startups are all about creating value, and
specifically creating value from little or nothing, from a
raw start, you need to have a frame of mind that is funda-

mentally optimistic, where you feel you can have an impact and where you feel you can change the way things are in a fundamental way. That takes a lot of confidence. If I look at the startups I've been in, and the many startups I've seen, there are always quite a number of things that happen to test your resolve. For that reason entrepreneurs need to have single-mindedness, confidence, and absolute focus on succeeding, no matter what.

Q: Even those traits don't guarantee success. What does?

Rapperport: No, they don't guarantee it. But you also have to do a lot of things well. You have to do a good job of identifying a good idea. You have to raise money successfully, which involves selling your good idea to investors. You have to be able to build a team, which involves getting a group enthusiastic—even when there's almost nothing there. You have to have the ability to get your first customers. First customers come in because they trust you personally on some level and they do that because they think you're going to be able to succeed.

Q: How important is having the right first customer?

Rapperport: I was involved with a startup that did streaming radio content over the internet, VXtreme, which we started in '96. Microsoft bought us in the summer of '97. It was a relatively fast ramp-up. But we had a very good, big customer—CNN. We had a solution for streaming video over the Internet and some very good technology. We had a tremendous group of people. And we were in an extremely fast-moving space. Having an early "lighthouse" customer like CNN gave us very strong references and helped people believe in the company.

Q: How many people were involved in starting that company?

Rapperport: We had a team of six people. It was a set of technologists, and I was the first business person on the team.

Q: What are some of the other attributes you need to start a successful company? For instance, do you need a flash of inspiration? A "eureka" moment?

Rapperport: I don't think it has to be a "eureka" idea, but you have be well ahead of the pack. You have to be one of only a few groups that are focused on what will become a strong market. And, obviously, the fact that you're starting something means there might be wonderful things pushing it to become a market. But in some sense, almost by definition—at least in software—you have to start before there's a real market and then you have to start building. So there's a period where, almost by definition, you are ahead of the market. And if that period is too long, then you're not going to have the money it takes to be there when the market happens. And if that period is too short, others are going to have built a solution and will beat you when the market takes off. So there's a certain piece of it where you want to be in advance of the market, but not too much.

Q: That sounds very hard to calculate.

Rapperport: Yes, it's very hard to calculate. But there are lots and lots of ideas that, if executed well, will create a lot of value for all concerned. And I think so much of success or failure is simply executing well. In my current company, we have a great idea. I'm very pleased with it. But even if it was only a good idea and not a great one, a good idea, if executed well, is absolutely enough to succeed.

Q: Should startups have an exit strategy, going in? Should that be the focus? Or, should everybody be thinking, "We're going to be the next Microsoft and we're going to be around forever"?

Rapperport: I don't think that it has to be either of those choices. I think that you have to be focused, as I said, on creating value and building a company. If you do that, then there will be exit strategies presenting themselves. You're going to have choices regarding what makes sense in any given period in your evolution. By determining an exit strategy before you start, you're just narrowing your choices unnecessarily. And to some extent, you're devoting mind share to something that isn't associated with growing the business. You're actually thinking about how to get out of the business, not how to grow the business. Growing the business should take all of your mental energy. You don't want to be distracted.

Q: What are some other success factors you can point to?

Rapperport: In software, there's a huge emphasis on the team. So I think a team, whether it's just plain better than the other guy's team, is very, very important and hugely increases your chances of success. If you look at why startups don't work, to a very, very high degree it's because the team doesn't work together for whatever reason, or it's made up of a group of people who aren't very talented.

Q: How do you build the right team?

Rapperport: It's really just intuitive. Part of what you're doing as an entrepreneur is getting a collection of people who you're going to work with, that you feel like you can work with, someday. The personality of the entrepreneur, or the partners if it's a partnership, is going to have a huge impact on the type of people hired. You're going to get a different culture, depending on who's hired. In fact, the culture is going to be reflective of the entrepreneur, more or less.

But you also have to be extremely careful to do a lot of due diligence to make sure you get to know the people who you're looking to bring in well before you hire them. That means a lot of interviews, lots of talking to references. And I believe in getting a pretty wide cross section of references. I say that you have to be careful because that first group of people you bring in is going to determine to a huge degree whether or not you succeed.

Q: How important is the board to a startup's success?

Rapperport: Well, you need a board that works effectively. In startups, in my experience, you have to have board meetings once a month. Board meetings are an opportunity to have a serious discussion regarding business issues. They aren't rap sessions. The board has to be engaged. It has to work.

I've had very good success with VCs on the board. We have three of them on our board now. One good thing about VCs on the board is they've seen a lot of startup companies. They have a pretty good sense of what works and are able to identify patterns and other things early. After VCs, you need to have functional expertise. Some VCs may be able to give you that or you may have to go outside and get other people.

But boards shouldn't be directive. They should be a group of people who are very in touch with what you're doing as a business and whose opinion you respect. So it's really like a conversation you're having with a group of people who care a lot about your business and are up to date. I would be concerned if the board becomes too directive. If it does, it sounds dangerous to me. I say that because at the end of the day, the board isn't going to be as close to the business as management is. So the board should be a group you're having a dialogue with. If strategic issues are being decided by the board on an ongoing basis, I would say you probably have an issue with the way the operating management team is working.

———

WALKING A FINE LINE

Not surprising, the expanding role of directors raises red flags among entrepreneurs and investors. There is a fine line between board oversight and actual involvement in managing a company. Boards that are involved in direct management of a company, some say, are too close and are overstepping their bounds. Boards need to understand the separation of church and state, as it were, or manager and overseer, as the case may be.

But our research revealed that hands-on directors can be value-creators in a startup environment, depending on the specific stage of a startup's existence. Successful startups are able to gauge when to shift or add new board members, depending on the business and growth needs of the young company. Since the venture capital community was born in the 1950s in Silicon Valley, VCs have occupied board seats for startup companies. Legendary venture pioneers like Arthur Rock, Don Valentine, Tommy Davis, and John Doerr played significant roles in the birth and development of some of the industry's greatest success stories, from Intel to Apple to Sun Microsystems to Google.

Investors often decide the fate of their ventures. For example, Kalpana, an Ethernet switching startup, was struggling in the early 1990s as it sought the right management mix. An angel investor named Jim Jordan came in as the new chief executive, replaced the entire management team, and then, despite the board's desire to file an IPO, sold the company to Cisco Systems in 1994.

The new management team concentrated on fixing product development problems and creating a product roadmap for the future. Having grabbed a large portion of the nascent Ethernet switching market, Kalpana was well positioned for an IPO. According to Charles Giancarlo, a member of the new management team, Jordan, who had several successful startups under his belt, abhorred the idea of working for a public company. As the dominant personality and a key investor, Jordan negotiated with IBM for months before accepting an offer from Cisco.

"Once Jim took over, the board pretty much stepped out in terms of day-to-day management," Giancarlo recalls. "Jim likes to run a company his own way, and the investors had essentially put all their eggs in his basket. And after the first six months, the company started to perform extremely well and growth was very good. There wasn't much for the board to do to help."

In selling Kalpana to Cisco, Jordan had frustrated his board, which felt a public offering would yield far more lucrative returns. Though Jordan left after the acquisition, a significant number of Kalpana's management team stayed on at Cisco, including Giancarlo, who is now an executive vice president.

HOW LONG IS TOO LONG?

While having investors on boards is standard, the presence of VCs on boards is not without controversy. As startups evolve from seed stage to survival mode and into sustained growth and a possible IPO or acquisition, VCs and CEOs are more likely to clash or find themselves with different agendas. Such friction can cause disruption and even sink a venture before it reaches a successful outcome.

Entrepreneurs complain that the VCs are focused on an exit strategy, seeking liquidity as early as possible in order to maximize the payoff to limited partners. Given that this is the VC's business, such focus is fully expected. But if the management team has grander, longer-term plans, the opportunity for conflict arises.

"Our venture guys stood by the company and helped it get to where it was," says Mike DeFranza, founder and CEO of Captivate Networks, a technology startup in Westford, Massachusetts. "I have nothing bad to say about them. But you need to recognize the fact that they have different agendas. They're there to maximize the return on investment. You're there to build a company. Sometimes those two agendas conflict."

As startups move beyond the seed stage, the nascent company requires business focus and the creation of sound business processes and discipline to go forward. Sooner than later, these needs will not be filled by the VCs and the board must find new members with a variety of skills.

Coyne's experience at Akamai embodies the way young companies must rethink their boards. Coyne joined Akamai's board in 2001 while he was executive vice president at Kodak, where he ran the company's $9 billion film division, which made up 70 percent of Kodak's revenues. This big company wisdom would be invaluable to a startup.

Coyne had begun his own personal development plan, seeking to learn more about the Internet and where the digital world was headed when he came upon Akamai. At age fifty-five, he had decided to embrace semiretirement, join four boards, and "enjoy life." But his work on boards was not intended to be a time-filler. He believed that he could bring big-company focus and process to startups, and as a professional director devote the necessary time and energy to make a difference.

At the time, Akamai still had two of its original venture capitalists on the board, but CEO George Conrades was taking steps to expand the board and add people with specific business skills. Conrades's idea was to bring in needed business acumen while at the same time expand Akamai's customer base through influential new directors.

After Coyne had been on the board for more than a year, most of which he spent quietly observing, he emerged as the voice of reason and experience, an objective outsider with a large-company resume who hadn't experienced the bubble firsthand. But he had enough business wisdom to see that Akamai was a prototype for startups in a crucial transition. Coyne eventually became Akamai's lead director and has, according to Conrades, played a key role in the growth of the company.

Startups, Coyne says, must go through a series of cultural changes: the brilliant idea, the vision, the resulting euphoria, the complete commitment of the founders and early employees, the willingness to do whatever it takes to succeed, acting quickly and aggressively. "Smart entrepreneurs are open to disagreeing with each other, and they want quick results," Coyne says of a young company. "They don't want to waste six months. They want to kill something today. It's all the qualities you'd like in an entrepreneurial startup."

After a year Coyne wondered what he was doing at Akamai. He wasn't adding value and felt that he was sitting in the "midst of a war." The board meetings were highly acrimonious as the VCs were focused on raising the stock price and fashioning a profitable exit. Arguments tended to focus on how much revenue the company received from a specific customer and why it was not as high as anticipated. Coyne was stunned as directors and managers debated about a customer spending $10,000 rather than $18,000 for the month instead of concentrating on the negative cash flow that would mean bankruptcy within fourteen months.

Though venture capitalists will make the case for their presence on boards, Coyne believes that the focus on an early exit eventually becomes detrimental to a startup's success. The behavior, while predictable, is not conducive to creating the discipline and process a startup requires for long-term viability.

In the end, the VCs left the board and Conrades sought new directors from various industry sectors to intensify the focus on business issues. In October 2002, faced with negative cash flow, negative earnings, and a continuing nightmarish information technology marketplace, Akamai's board asked the question: "How do we survive?"

BEYOND SURVIVAL

Among the first targets was cash flow. The board pushed hard on this issue. Coyne vocally asserted that a stake had to be put into the ground and that the company could simply not go below $100 million in the bank. That decision set off a cascade of painful actions, including a major downsizing of the company.

Because Akamai went public quickly during the Internet bubble and experienced the runup of its share price to $345, the company behaved like a wide-eyed child in a candy store. Money was spent like water. Expensive office space was leased at ridiculous prices during the height of the boom. The company overhired, staffing as if it was a $500 million company when its revenues were nowhere near that level. The startup was hemorrhaging cash.

By picking a number as a baseline, the board gave Akamai marching orders and insisted that action be taken. Management had to confront the truth. Standard answers such as "We'll raise revenue. We'll sell more. We'll increase our gross margin so we don't have to cut so much" were cast aside. Hard decisions that had been put off now had to be made. People had to be laid off, leases broken, downsizing endured.

The layoffs, as always, were deeply painful, even traumatic. But the board refused to budge. No other course was considered. Coyne had done his own budget reviews and knew that human nature tempted managers to try to sugarcoat the top line with promises of better margins and higher sales. But instead the goal became discipline on a level the company had not previously adopted.

Instead of "How much did we sell to Nike last month?" the board asked, "How many customers did we gain? How many did we lose? What was the average revenue per customer? And what do we have in the pipeline that will close in the next 30 days, 90 days, 120 days," and so on. An unusual rolling fifteen-month fiscal plan was instituted so that management would have a "fifth quarter" in which it could extrapolate how each quarter was shaping up and how realistic the plans and expectations for the near-term future might be.

At every meeting the board asked pointed questions of management. "You said you were going to sell $10 million in new business in the next quarter, but only sold $7 million. Where did you fall short and why?" No one had asked these questions before. The boom-and-bust cycle of the bubble had consumed everyone's attention, and management was scrambling to keep Akamai afloat. But sooner or later, as a company like Akamai emerges from survival mode into the promise of long-term viability, a new key question crops up, longing for an answer: "Now that we know we are going to survive, what do we want to be when we grow up?"

Coyne put a set of priorities in place and pushed for attention to be paid to several key issues, including succession planning. Though this may well be a backburner issue for early-stage companies, the idea made sense at Akamai. Conrades was sixty-five in 2004 and was surrounded by a cast of highly talented, highly motivated technical people in their late twenties and early thirties. If the company was to move from survival mode to growth mode, it was essential that the company develop its young talent, immerse them in management functions, managing people, assessing and developing talent, and making them ready to become leaders.

"If you want to grow the business from $150 million to, say, $1 billion, you need a cadre of very seasoned managers and leaders," Coyne says. "You've got to turn that raw talent—rookies with phenomenal potential—into a winning team."

Like all the companies in our research, Akamai remains a work in progress. The fruits of the board's aggressive style have already been born, but the company's long-term fortunes are as yet unknown. One thing is clear: without the board's heavy-handed involvement, Akamai may well have failed already.

GOVERNANCE, NOT MANAGEMENT

Despite activist board members like Coyne, venture capitalists remain cautious about the role of boards in startups. "A good board is about governance, not management," declares Alex Osadzinski, a partner in Trinity Ventures.

For most VCs, a board's role should be strategic, focusing on markets, customers, pricing, and channels, and drawing on the board's collective experience. To them, if a board gets too close to the policy-making, price-setting, hiring, and operations, it has crossed a dangerous line into management. "That means the CEO is not doing the job anymore," Osadzinski says.

Boards should not be overestimated or underestimated, he adds. If the management team is weak or the idea is bad, no amount of board input will fix a startup. In addition, no matter how strong a board is, if the CEO refuses to work with the directors, a startup will suffer.

Given the myriad personality types that VCs encounter among entrepreneurs, the path to value and success may be as much psychotherapy as business counseling. Wade Woodson, a partner at Sigma Partners, a venture firm in Menlo Park, points out that boards ideally act as partners with management. Boards encounter ego-driven CEOs, for example, for whom a title is more paramount than cooperating to create a successful venture.

"I have more of a problem with people who are in it for ego than those who are in it for a financial return for themselves and their families," Woodson says. "Our job is to work with them and have an opinion about what is right for the company and work to achieve it. If you have a CEO who is taking the company down, it is your responsibility to your investors and everyone who works there to fix it."

Though stories circulate about venture firms who torpedo management, Woodson says that most management teams are long aware of the need for change at the top by the time the board acts. "I have never seen a situation where we took out a CEO and put in a new one where the rest of the team didn't say, 'It's about time. How come you guys have been asleep at the switch?'" Woodson says.

The VCs acknowledge that exit strategies are a priority in their involvement with the startup. But they argue that the label given VCs as short-term opportunists is a myth. Osadzinski, who was an entrepreneur before joining Trinity Ventures, says that he had always believed that if a VC could double his money in a year, "they would flip the company just like that." Such thinking among investors is not true, he insists.

"If you asked most limited partners whether they'd rather have $2 million back in a year on a $1 million investment or $5 million in five years, they'll tell you $5 million in five years," he says.

Osadzinski acknowledges that as investors, VCs must protect their limited partners and seek the highest and fastest return. But with that said, the commitment to success is paramount. Boards should not be comprised entirely of VCs. VCs—especially top-tier, experienced VCs—desire mixed, diverse boards with outside directors to achieve balance and a diversity of views.

In the end, Osadzinski echoes what most investors believe about startups. Boards must be aligned. They must be invested, involved, and interested. Boards that are not aligned signal trouble within the venture, and success becomes fleeting. In addition, the CEO and his team must be willing to work with the board. "Good teams and good boards work very well," he says. "Everything else is just a pain."

As we will see in the next set of chapters, the resources metric in our research plays a key role in the success of startups. Given all the intellectual capacity of strong boards, a startup can't really hope to survive without getting a forceful running start in generating and controlling cash flow.

———

## Five

Cash Flow:
Show Me the Money

For a startup to have much hope for long-term success, managing cash flow competently is table stakes to the game. Though some would assume this path to value is simple and intuitive, it is anything but. If the Internet bubble taught us anything, it is that keeping a tight and disciplined hand on the burn rate is crucial to a young company's future.

Our research confirmed that successful startups showed strong cash flow throughout their financing rounds, even in the early rounds. These standouts were earning revenues while effectively managing expenses and were close to break-even or positive cash flow by their later rounds.

Yet managing cash flow remains a daunting task for many startups for a variety of reasons. When the bubble burst in 2000 and venture financing all but disappeared, there was a widespread presumption that lessons had been learned, and if the marketplace ever got reenergized, entrepreneurs and investors would be chastened, humbled, and ready to demonstrate fiscal discipline. Yet there are signs that the emergence of new venture funding has been accompanied by bubble logic: the more funding available, the freer the spending, the faster the burn rate.

A report in the *Boston Globe* in August 2004 noted that smaller companies were raising $8 million to $10 million in early-stage deals, which was up from $5 million to $7 million in the years since the bubble burst. Tom Crotty, a general partner at Battery Ventures, a VC firm in Wellesley, Massachusetts, worried that the increase in funding could be a harbinger of a return to the ill-fated bubble thinking.

"It could signal a loss of discipline in terms of managing cash efficiently," Crotty said. "I'm afraid people are forgetting the lessons of the bubble. There could be a train wreck coming if we're not careful."

Although we acknowledge the constraints and foibles of human nature, we believe that the most successful startups not only learned the lessons but probably would have been among those with fiscal focus and discipline regardless of the bubble.

WHAT WE FOUND

Our research, for example, revealed that:

- The more successful companies scored higher in the cash flow metric during later rounds of financing and in higher customer acquisition scores for all rounds.

- There is a strong correlation between customer acquisition and cash flow. In other words, these startups were raising capital to accelerate growth rather than simply to meet expenses.

- Less successful companies had a higher cash flow in the seed round and then saw it decline. Too much high-level staff ate up cash.

Positive cash flow, on the face of it, is a straightforward quest. Startups, particularly venture-funded startups, are aware from the outset that investor expectations include the swift climb to revenues that exceed expenses.

In this there is the danger of being venture funded. Most venture capitalists have deadlines that require startups to get things moving as quickly as possible. Decisions based on accelerating cash flow, accelerating growth, and finding a quicker exit strategy are not necessarily conducive to building a sustainable business for the long haul. Some young companies follow their dreams without venture funding and find that, if successful, there are capital markets interested in funding growth. The conventional wisdom in the startup world has always been that *the best time to raise money is when you don't need it.* A company that does not have a sustainable business plan, no matter how much capital is infused early on, has a tougher time surviving.

CASH FLOW IS KING

Our research confirmed another bit of conventional wisdom: cash flow is an issue of discipline and focus. Unless a startup is over-funded, there is simply no excuse for losing sight of the crucial balance between income and capital expenditures. The beauty and allure of startups is that they are small, have few people, and have fewer layers of complexities and stresses than large organizations. Yet it is not clear that startups naturally display fiscal discipline. One assumes that the lack of abundant cash automatically instills discipline. In fact, resource constraints ought to lead to fiscal discipline, and often does. But recent memory is tainted by startups that were loaded with cash but lost their fiscal compass. People start doing foolish things: overpaying themselves and other employees, leasing opulent office space, investing in unnecessary overhead.

In fact, we learned another simple bit of wisdom: successful entrepreneurs are smart at squeezing risk out of the equation. The mythical Silicon Valley cowboys who thrive on risk and land massive rewards are either relics of the bubble or never truly existed. Smart entrepreneurs look to mitigate risk, to lower risk rather than raise it.

Financial health is critical for a startup. When employees get wind of financial troubles, they are unlikely to remain as committed and passionate as they had been. Partners are less likely to enter agreements or live up to existing agreements. Competitors circle like sharks with blood in the water and use such knowledge to win business. Customers are wary of signing deals with financially strapped startups.

IMPORTANT QUESTIONS

Cash in actuality is a stand-in for the other things required to reach important milestones in a new business. Entrepreneurs need to ask themselves:

- How well are you managing cash?
- Are you forecasting it accurately?
- Do you know when you'll run out of money?
- Is there a strategy in place to extend the cash if you need it?

Smart managers are in control of these factors and have a sense of when to turn the dial to either increase or decrease the cash burn. During market downturns, as the recent recession demonstrated, most startups get caught in the deepest water without a life preserver. Alex Osadzinski of Trinity Ventures has seen the dangers of such experiences.

"Most companies, as they see the market come down, think it is just a dent and they keep spending," he says. "And then 'whoops, we're out of money.' There's always less money and less time than you think. And the good teams know that."

Osadzinski has a simple formula for calculating cash burn. A startup burning a million dollars a month and firmly in the black feels comfortable that it has at least ten months of run rate, which it considers nearly a year. In fact, in four months, it is down to a six-month run rate.

"And by then, if they haven't started raising their next $10 million, they're not going to get it. So that ten months of run rate is actually four," Osadzinski explains. Panic tends to set in, and the company starts to throttle back spending and costs itself two or three months' time to grow the business, which could then leave it only a matter of weeks to find new funding.

With the pressure of achieving positive cash flow, managers of startup companies often must make difficult, sometimes treacherous decisions, about where to focus resources, how to dole out spending, and how to set priorities.

CASH FLOW MUST MATCH STRATEGY

One CEO in our research spoke about an experience raising a round of financing a year earlier. The company's high-tech software offering was suitable for several industry sectors, but the venture capitalists pushed hard for the startup to concentrate on a single industry. The CEO reluctantly heeded this advice and settled on the utility sector. Fourteen months later, the company experienced an unexpected truth about utilities: they are notoriously slow to make technology-buying decisions. Closing deals had become tortuous and infrequent. The investors insisted on accompanying the firm's sales team on a customer call, which went badly, and afterward they told the CEO that he wouldn't be seeing another dime from the VCs.

Dismayed because the company was burning through its cash, the CEO replied, "You told us to focus on one market. You forced us to follow this strategy." The investors acknowledged that the company had done everything right, but had simply made the wrong choice of industries.

What this anecdote suggests is that cash flow must be constantly matched with the strategic objective of the company, regardless of what investors are telling the entrepreneurs. Sometimes it is worth spending an extra three months choosing the right strategy for scaling up. Many startups scale up without having chosen the right target upon which to scale and run into a wall. Recovery is extremely difficult. Getting experience and strategic thinking into the budget is crucial and reinforces what we discussed in the earlier chapter on boards and their influence.

At Akamai, George Conrades and his team learned the hard way about cash flow. Flush with cash from a successful early IPO, the company, as noted earlier, leased high-priced Cambridge office space, hired with abandon, and took on all the trappings of a high-flying bubble boomer. When the bubble burst, Akamai faced the trauma of instilling unfamiliar fiscal discipline, a decision made by a new and aggressive board. As part of the new discipline, the company had to lay off nearly half its workforce and move into cheaper quarters.

Conrades echoes what CEOs of most startups believe: the metrics had always been in place, but the smart CEO knows which metric to emphasize. Early on, for example, Akamai spent $10 million to install an enterprise-wide Siebel information technology package. Though the system became an integral part of the operation, it was an expensive choice for a five-year-old company.

So when reality set in postbubble, the company had to begin making intelligent spending decisions because "the VC money will run out; even the money we raised in the IPO will run out," Conrades explains. "We had to do a convertible bond offering." With the board now riding herd on the cash flow issue, the company implemented budgets and reconsidered even the smallest details. No more free vending machines, no more free pizza and snacks. People now pay fifty cents for a can of Coke. Conrades estimates that the company spent several hundred thousand dollars a year on the giveaways. "People were taking the stuff home anyway," he says.

One of the benefits of a financial crisis is that once threatened with the company's extinction, people jump on board quickly. "The more dire your straits become, the easier it is to communicate why we were making changes and why we are charging at the vending machines, why cell phone usage had to come down, and why we weren't buying a new laptop every year for everybody," Conrades says. "It's always better to do that against the backdrop of an emergency so there's a reason that everybody understands and goes along with. What you don't want to do is put that stuff back in place, even if things get better. Instead, it just becomes part of the culture."

With the small stuff now under control, Akamai keeps a close eye on the critical capital costs as well.

"We became stingy about adding headcount," Conrades says. "We are really chary about adding headcount and if we can find a way to do it differently, we do. Wouldn't it be great if we can set a goal of being a multibillion-dollar revenue company but never have more than 750 people? It's possible if you work at it. If you don't think that way, you say, 'Well, we're growing. Let's add another hundred people. We'll just parse it out among the departments.' That is the worst thing you can do. Right there is the beginning of the end."

FUNDING THE RIGHT CHOICES

The choices are not always easy or intuitive. Jump-starting cash flow is essential for startups, but how they react to the lure of nonstrategic cash is likely to have an impact on future success. For example, a software startup is often asked by its first customers to help with implementation. Is it a bad idea or good idea to take your core development team and send them out into the field to handle such implementations?

On one hand, the experience is invaluable in providing the team with direct exposure to how the product is being used. It also can bring in substantial revenues for the company. But it also can distract key people and delay the overall development of the product. This scenario is common for software startups that must decide how to respond to such challenges in order to survive. The decision cannot be made ad hoc, customer by customer, because expectations of the company's business model are set from the very beginning. Many choose to view themselves as service companies, but services companies are generally not as scalable as product companies.

Yuchun Lee of Unica Software is a devoted student of business history. When he founded Unica, he carefully studied a list of successful software startups that had reached $1 billion in sales. Looking at their cash flow metrics Lee discovered that there was a consistent theme: they all became profitable very early on.

"No company lost money when their revenue hit $15 million, which is a very small amount," Lee says. "Many of them raised very little money; in fact, some raised zero money all the way through to the IPO."

The startups had high gross margins at the same time as high growth rates and cash generation. "People say, 'Oh, you can't do that. It's against the laws of physics. If you grow fast, you've got to burn cash.' It's just not true," Lee says.

Entrepreneurs tend to get confused about what should be a clear goal: building a successful company. Lee points out that if the single objective is to bring in revenue, that's one type of business. "But if your objective is to build a successful company, that's another type of business," he explains. If the latter is your goal, "being able to manage cash while you grow has to be part and parcel of your plan. If your model is not fine-tuned to generate cash and be profitable, how can you expect to suddenly grow up and say, 'Now we're going to be profitable'?"

BENCHMARKING THE FIELD

Startups need to benchmark themselves against public companies when those companies were small. What were the expense levels? How much did they spend on R&D? How much did they spend on general administration (GNA)?

Lee prides himself on Unica's fiscal discipline throughout its history. He acknowledges that in 1999 Unica was growing at 140 percent, and this put some pressure on the cash flow side. So Lee went to a couple of venture firms for a round of financing. As stated earlier, the best time to seek funding is when you don't need it. The company raised cash in 1999 and 2001, but it was more as a hedge, a cushion so that management wouldn't have to worry about being caught short in the cash flow area as growth accelerated. "All that money is still in the bank," Lee says. "We haven't used it."

He also understands how his advice is easy to give, harder to follow. Two or three competitors did not survive the recession because they simply ran out of cash. "If you build a company that can generate cash, then you can ride through the weak times," Lee says. "But generating cash is hard because you've got to make tough judgment calls."

Our research suggests that although many early-stage companies have not yet achieved cash flow break-even, revenues are an important indicator of the company's potential to fill a market niche. Thus it is difficult to reject revenue-generating opportunities. But the savvy CEO will navigate these tough decisions with clarity and strong leadership, finding ways to balance the young company's resources without undermining its core activities.

A CASH FLOW STRESS TEST

There are various techniques of good cash management, strong forecasting, and having a sense of when to turn the dials on spending. How stingy must a company be with invested capital before it becomes penny-wise and pound foolish? Our research revealed that successful startups are often tested financially—a type of cash flow stress test, if you will—which provides the kind of battle experience that helps render better long-term decision making.

A good cash flow stress test should ask:

- Has a startup always had enough capital? Or has it been through periods where no one got paid for three months and made it through anyway? For venture investors, this can be a significant test of the team's commitment moving forward.

- How did the team respond when there was little cash? Was there dissension and finger-pointing or did they calmly maneuver through the white water? This kind of survival training tests the mettle of the core team members in ways that may prove critical down the road.

What most entrepreneurs eventually discover is that cash flow is simply an indicator, not a true measure, of value of a new company. If a startup has nine months left of cash, what is it doing to create value in those nine months? How is the cash flow issue affecting priorities? Resources and strategic priorities are inextricably intertwined and inevitably lead to the source of value creation.

Eric Ingersoll is CEO of Mechanology, a startup in Attleboro, Massachusetts, that develops industrial compressors using new technology. As CEO of a nascent enterprise, he is trying to build awareness of the true value of the company. "Our bare bones burn rate is between $75,000 and $80,000 per month," Ingersoll says. "I try to impart to our team that if we can do something that shortens our time frame to key milestones by one month, it is worth hundreds of thousands of dollars, not just $80,000. If you think of your startup as having an opportunity to be a $100 million player within three years, or whatever measure you use, you can figure out how much each month is worth. If a company is creating value, it is worth vastly more than the money you are putting into it."

In other words, teams must understand the true nature of value. "People can get so concerned about managing cash and extending the burn rate that they are not actually prioritizing things that create value in the company," Ingersoll says.

The good news is that capital efficiency seems to be returning to the prebubble-era thinking. As startups now understand, a strong dose of fiscal reality goes a long way in getting heads and budgets on straight.

As we will see in the next chapter, strategy metrics such as market size, competitive position, and business model are deeply intertwined with the wise and capable oversight of cash flow.

Six

———

You Can Only Grow as Big as Your Market

The strategy axes of our research include market size, competitive position, and business model. These three metrics—which relate to how a startup fits into the world it is trying to penetrate—are vital for an entrepreneur's chances for success. Market size is important because it represents a cap on potential sales volume. Competitive position can be protected by patents or other types of temporary monopoly and will dictate the company's ability to add value for investors. The business model is among the most crucial metrics because it allows a startup to create not only a sound pricing model but a foundation for how it will do business.

In the strategy axes of our research, we discovered that market size is both a critical but nonintuitive factor in the path to value for startups. Estimating market size can be more art than science, and we found that larger markets, whether actual or perceived at the early stages of financing, are not necessarily an advantage for a startup. Some less successful companies reported very high estimates of market size and raised significant amounts of money in an attempt to penetrate these allegedly large markets. Conversely, companies that initially targeted smaller markets often achieved lower scores on this axis, but were able to manage growth and add more value over time.

We found:

- Less successful software startups focused on what they perceived (or hoped) to be very large markets. As a result of this misperception, these companies never reached sufficient customer, revenue, and business model traction.

- The more successful services companies focused on narrow markets early, avoiding the misperceptions about market size that plagued their less successful competitors.

TOO MUCH OF A GOOD THING

Yuchun Lee's experience at Unica Software echoes our research findings. Most successful companies—in his case, in the enterprise software space—despite projected market size, don't raise a lot of money up front but become profitable quickly. "In our business, money actually doesn't help, it actually hurts," Lee says. "There are lots of examples where companies raised just tons of money and grew rapidly, but they never knew how to make money. They carried that mistake with them through the next phase of growth, and because they were never profitable, they couldn't build a sustainable business. They either got bought out or they flame out by running out of cash. We've seen that a lot in our industry."

Lee did extensive research into billion-dollar software firms and noted that there was consistency in this blueprint. Many of these successful target companies raised very little venture money. Many had high gross margins at the same time as a high growth rate and the ability to generate cash. "A lot of people say, 'That's impossible. It's against the laws of physics; if you grow fast, you've got to burn cash!'" Lee says. "But that's simply not true for successful software companies."

So contrary to popular belief, venture money in some industries is actually not helpful. Therefore, market size can be both a blessing and a curse depending on how a startup embraces and explores its target market.

"The wisdom comes from the marketplace," says Amiel Kornel, the Silicon Valley–based senior managing director at Spencer Trask & Company. Our research confirms that the most successful startups take a strong, proactive stance on determining the validity of the marketplace by immersing themselves in the market as they are developing their concepts and their technology. Rather than holding good ideas close to the vest, the smartest entrepreneurs are out asking questions, having discussions with potential customers, analyzing trends, and sharing their ideas with the very market they hope to enter or create.

Indeed, the venture capital community has grown reluctant, especially after the dot-com meltdown, to accept entrepreneurs' estimates of market size at their word. "Every market is a billion dollars," Trinity Ventures' Alex Osadzinski says sarcastically. "The big question is: what is really going on in that market space? I've worked in markets that are 'multibillion dollars' and you can't identify where the market is. For example, I worked in the enterprise application integration market, which is generally accepted by analysts to be a $15 billion market. But I'm damned if I can find more than $2 billion starting with the revenues of all the vendors in it."

SOLVE A PROBLEM AND THE MONEY WILL FOLLOW

Companies in our research spanned a wide array of entrepreneurial zeal, from those that moved a technology or service forward incrementally to those who sought to create entirely new markets. Those in the latter category tend to be less risk averse, more adventuresome but laser focused. Solve a problem for someone, they believe, and there will always be money. Focus on the value, the impact of the technology instead of the technology itself, and the market will likely emerge. Such is the case with Captivate Network, Inc., a startup that literally has gone up and down.

In 1996, Michael DiFranza, now the CEO of Captivate, was a young technology executive looking for the next new thing. After returning to Boston on a red-eye flight from the West Coast, DiFranza stopped by his downtown office to pick up some work. He stepped into the elevator in the high-rise office tower and, despite his jetlag haze, DiFranza couldn't help but notice the other people around him. As he leaned against the back wall of the elevator, he could see the visible discomfort of his fellow passengers. They fidgeted, looked at their watches, stared at the floor numbers as each was lit sequentially, anything to avoid eye contact with each other.

By the time DiFranza stepped off the elevator, an idea had formulated in his mind. What if you put a flat panel display inside the elevator and fed continuous programming to it so that elevator passengers had something to watch on their vertical journeys? Could you calculate the market size, the audience, and possibly sell advertising to accompany the programming?

A recent stint at the Program for Management Development at the Harvard Business School had set DiFranza off on a search for a new idea for a startup, and now he believed he had one. When he sat down with some colleagues to think through his new concept, the first question that required an answer was: Is there a market, and how big will it be?

DiFranza's eureka moment eventually morphed into Captivate Network, Inc. Ride an elevator in an office tower in New York, Boston, Chicago, Los Angeles, Atlanta, Toronto, Vancouver, San Francisco, and a growing list of other cities and you are likely to see a Captivate screen delivering a stream of weather, traffic, financial updates, sports, and news, along with advertising.

Captivate beat substantial odds, survived the dot-com bubble and subsequent recession, and eventually was acquired by Gannett, the media giant, in 2004. The company estimates that it reaches 1.4 million viewers each day in such prestigious properties as the Empire State Building, the Sears Tower, and the Prudential Center in Boston. It has attracted a vast array of advertisers, including IBM, McDonald's, Yahoo!, Lexus, Sony, Staples, and many more who are willing to pay advertising dollars to reach the captive elevator audience.

A series of crucial management decisions led to Captivate's ultimate success, but identifying and analyzing a market—in this case, an untapped market—was the first crucial step to glory.

DiFranza and his startup team faced three hurdles from the outset: building a viable delivery system for their programming, convincing real estate companies of the value of installing such equipment, and perhaps most challenging, convincing advertisers that this was an effective way to reach out to consumers.

In order to determine the market, DiFranza had to decide early on what kind of a company Captivate would be: a technology company or a media company. Although it created the wireless hardware and software required to deliver its targeted programming, Captivate's success stemmed from recognizing its opportunity as a media company.

FINDING THE AUDIENCE, KNOWING THE AUDIENCE

Using media-based metrics Captivate identified its audience as a demographic: $100,000 average income versus $54,000 for the general population, managerial, professional, difficult to reach, fifty/fifty split between female and male. It was, in fact, the same audience targeted by the *Wall Street Journal*, *BusinessWeek*, *Fortune*, and *Forbes*.

"When we started the company, it was in the middle of the Internet boom," DiFranza says, "and we recognized that advertisers were looking for efficient and effective ways to reach out to customers. We felt we could offer the value proposition that we bring an exceptional audience to the advertising community. Because we are not a broadcast medium, we don't reach everybody. Instead, we reach a very well-defined, targeted, high-end demographic that can't be reached through traditional means in an efficient way."

Not only that but Captivate would be reaching these consumers during the workday when they are making buying decisions for their companies and themselves.

According to a Nielsen Media Research survey, the average person in an office tower takes six elevator trips per day, with each trip averaging a minute. These are top to bottom rides—interfloor trips were not counted—so Captivate concluded that the average person was spending 120 minutes a month, twenty-four hours a year riding in an elevator.

Using an advertising model, Captivate sells space based on ad buys—each ad will run once every ten minutes for a month, for example—and they calculate that based on that frequency, 100 percent of the audience will see the ad twelve times over a one-month period. "There is no other medium that can guarantee that level of exposure," DiFranza says.

Because this was a completely virgin market, Captivate didn't have the luxury of comparing itself to market leaders. It had to not only shape the market but convince customers that such a market existed. Proving its value was no easy task. As a new medium, Captivate was held to a higher standard by the advertising community. In fact, according to DiFranza, Captivate's claims were considered lies until proven otherwise.

So the company hired Nielsen Media Research and paid $200,000 to receive research and data. "It was a big financial investment for a small company like us," DiFranza says. "But we had to bite the bullet so they could validate our audience for the advertisers."

Simultaneously, Captivate had to convince real estate companies of the inherent value of the new technology and create partnerships by offering a percentage of revenues from the installed systems. No sooner had Captivate begun to gain visibility then Otis Elevators decided to enter the nascent market itself, creating daunting competition, but at the same time validating the promise of the concept.

Over time, Captivate has conducted up to fifty of its surveys, each result surpassing client expectations. Otis's efforts, however, stalled, and it eventually became a Captivate partner. As more buildings opted to install the system, advertising revenues steadily grew. Now there are more than 4,500 screens installed, and Captivate provides a steady stream of programming offered by an impressive group of media partners, including CNN, the *New York Times,* the *Wall Street Journal,* and The Weather Channel.

Since 9/11, during one of the worst advertising economies in history, Captivate grew by 80 percent and the company raised more than $100 million in venture capital before being acquired by Gannett. Once-skeptical real estate companies now clamor for the technology, and a novel idea has already become ubiquitous.

The company's growth during the recession and eventual successful exit via acquisition have more than validated DiFranza's original vision.

FINDING A MARKET BEFORE IT IS A MARKET

For startups, specifically in the software and services sectors, determining market size, establishing the quickest route to sales, market share, and profits is often a daunting proposition. For example, in the software arena, there are generally two options: creating an entirely new market or entering an existing market with incrementally better technology.

———

RON BERNAL

Partner, Sutter Hill Ventures

Q: When you make an investment, how important is the exit strategy? Do you go into an investment thinking, this company would be a great acquisition target?

Bernal: Most of the venture guys, at least the high-quality ones I know, I don't think ever bet on that. They don't invest thinking somebody's going to acquire the company. When you go in and make an investment, you do it looking at the team, you go in analyzing the market, you go in looking for growth in the market. You go in saying, "Does this company have a chance of becoming a freestanding company?" But you don't go in saying, "Oh, this is going to be a two- or three-year thing and the most likely outcome will be an acquisition." You just don't do that.

Q: But isn't the rap on venture firms that they go into an investment looking for a quick exit?

Bernal: If you went back in time to the '80s or the first half of the '90s, everything was about building companies. During the bubble it changed because of the mercenary attitude of investors. They really did think about flipping companies, not about how they could build a company and real value. The high-tech community kind of went off course a little bit around the idea of what it meant to go into a startup. I'd say that was true for both the entrepreneurs and the VCs. I call that period the time of "drive-by financing." I will also tell you that it was all wrong. Surrealistic, in a way. I looked at 150 companies in '98 and, you know, there was just the feeling that if you didn't do something quick, you'd miss the boat. There was a feeling of velocity, and it was a gold rush mentality.

Q: Has it changed?

Bernal: I think we're going back to the future, so to speak. Back to the '80s and early '90s. People understand that in the end it's all about how you build value. They understand that you need patience to do that. I don't think there's the expectation that you can do everything you need to do in two years. At least that's my personal belief.

In the '80s, it was all about listening to the customer. Back then, I was at SGI, for about eight years. It was about that. It was all about using technology in a differentiated way. It was all about earning the right to do business with the customer. When I was at Cisco it was very much that way, too. We had a very customer-centric focus. I learned a valuable lesson from those two companies that I push pretty hard now with startups. I tell them you have to serve the customer. You can't just focus on technology. You really have to listen to your customer. You have to figure out what are the critical "pain points" for your customer and fix them. You have to provide your customer a solution that has high value.

I know this sounds a little bit like motherhood and apple pie, but a lot of companies don't really do that. They get wrapped up in [thinking that] their technology is everything. So even though the technology might be great, they kind of miss the point. After the bubble, another change I've seen is the return of the sales-oriented CEO, as opposed to the technology-based CEO.

Q: Is that part of the "back to the future" shift that you see going on?

Bernal: Yes. I think that's one of the more positive things to have happened in the aftermath of the bubble. I say that because I think it is all about serving the customer. It's amazing to me to watch Cisco, even with the amount of money they made: they remain humble, they remain willing to serve, to listen. As a result, Cisco is an extremely high learning organization, and it learns because it listens to its customers. It learns because they are very hard on themselves, because they have intellectual honesty.

So here's what I think are the hallmarks of really good, successful startups. You find a good-sized market and in that market you find some problems that are underserved. You then insert yourself into that market by serving customers' needs. By doing that you create a beachhead that you build out by continuously serving your customers. You do that in a value-added way, a differentiated way. But you do it by starting with the customer and serving the customer's needs.

Q: What traits does an entrepreneur need to do that?

Bernal: Intellectual honesty is the key. You can't start believing your own press. You also can't succumb to what I call the money disease. During the bubble—and it's a still a little bit true today—there was just too much money. Money tends to make you take your eye off the ball.

Q: Do you think the type of financing a company gets has an impact on its chances for success? Is there a difference between, say, angel financing and venture financing?

Bernal: I'm not real high on angel investing unless you really have what I call a professional angel who also really invests time, who's been through the journey before, who's going to put in significant time to help you build the company, because a lot of the guys will put money in. The same is true with companies. They have their own agendas, right? The only way I would ever let a strategic investor in is if it fit in as part of a business deal with them, which would give them the right to invest. I would not let them invest before they did a business deal.

I believe that you've got to get the smartest money you

can. In a way, everybody's money is great. But I tell people that whether you have angels or corporate or venture investors, too many people get focused on dilution. That's the wrong thing. The question is, if I have, say, two investors, do I get two firms and two different perspectives working for me to add value? To get and keep results? Do I have to get resources through all their connections? Will their networks—social, entrepreneurial, and so on—help me? That's more important than dilution.

Q: When you look at a company, what do you look for?

Bernal: We look at the management team. The management team probably has the highest correlation with the success of a company. Recently we looked at a company that had some great technology and unbelievable market potential. But we basically walked because of the CEO. We just asked ourselves whether this guy was the right guy to lead the company or whether he was just on a personal ego quest. That's why we walked.

The second thing we look at is probably the size of the market, of the business opportunity—and if that market is addressable.

Another thing we look at is whether the technology is defendable—whether it is a barrier to entry. What I like to see is a technology that creates a pretty high barrier to entry.

Let me add one other thing. During the bubble, people would say it's difficult to find good CEOs. They said they were a really scarce resource. I will tell you that today there's an even scarcer resource—someone who understands product management. By that I mean people who understand marketing, listening to customers, that can synthesize exactly what you have to do and how you position your product. That's a very difficult skill to find.

Q: Can you recall a time when you saw something—an idea, a company—and said, "Wow! I've just seen the future"?

Bernal: There have been several. But then when you start to think about it, you say, "Well, it will be very tough to develop the business, it's a pretty tight market, where are the distribution channels?"

———

Whether or not an entrepreneur is first or among the first, primary among their tasks is to identify an opportunity before it is a true market and then start building. Developing software for an emerging market so that product and market opportunity coincide is difficult at best. Hitting moving targets always is. The period when, by definition, a startup is ahead of the market can be stressful. Take too long to develop the product and cash flow becomes a significant problem, often sinking ventures before they are fully launched. Move too quickly and risk having competitors with better solutions strike just as the market takes off. Most successful startups are able to calculate the market-development phase well enough to reap the rewards, but only if they execute properly.

And as with any moving target, startups must be able to adapt and adjust their expectations and game plans on the fly. At Unica Software, founder Yuchun Lee had done exhaustive research and critical thinking about the market he wanted to enter. Launching an enterprise software startup, he reasoned, required some thoughtful calculations about an emerging but not brand-new marketplace. Having studied successful software launches he understood that there was more danger being the pioneer in enterprise software than in coming later to an already existing market.

Thus he took the road more easily traveled and began by licensing his data-mining technology to existing companies in a raft of industries. Not long into the venture, Lee realized he had to answer a fundamental question about the market: Should

Unica continue to be a horizontal player, selling not just market-ing automation but also manufacturing, process controls, cur-rency trading, drug discovery, and more, or should it focus on one application area?

"Around 1995, we decided to concentrate on one application area, enterprise marketing management, which was a pivotal turning point for the company," Lee says.

It takes a certain personality type for an entrepreneur to find personal fulfillment in being a latecomer to a burgeoning market. But for Lee, his sights were set on building a sustainable, indepen-dent company, not to stake a claim in the creation of new markets.

One of the advantages of entering an existing market with new and improved technology is that there are always some leading-edge customers eager to drive the product direction. Unica has al-ways displayed a knack for sensing correctly what the market needs and driving product development along that axis. "Being the second wave to the market, we're not reinventing any feature sets," Lee says. "We have RFPs coming to the door basically giv-ing us the spec for the product. Plus you have competitors' prod-ucts to look at as examples. We can spend our time figuring out how to be better as opposed to inventing new features that people might want."

Not surprising, our Star Charts tend to illustrate a low urgency for market size. In fact, in the software, services, and dot-com space, the most successful companies in this combined category showed higher scores on all value axes but two: market size and strength of the management team. These two categories were sig-nificantly higher for the less successful companies. The less suc-cessful companies perhaps overestimated their market size and might have overstaffed and accelerated their burn rates ahead of opportunity.

Although we've said already in this book that there is no single path to value but many paths to value, in the case of market size, this is especially true. Some venture capitalists will say, "Show me great markets, don't worry about the teams."

In the next chapter we will focus on competitive position. A startup, regardless of the market size it is targeting, will be unlikely to have significant impact if it hasn't mapped out where it stands vis-à-vis the competition.

———

## Seven

Moats, Walls, and Drawbridges: Maintaining Your Competitive Position Against the Fray

When Larry Page and Sergey Brin began to formulate their idea for a new online search engine in their Stanford dorm room, conventional wisdom should have convinced them that the competitive landscape would not support their dream. In 1998, when the young entrepreneurs launched Google, the Internet already had a surfeit of successful search engines, including Yahoo!, InfoSeek, Ask Jeeves, Excite, Hotbot, Lycos, AltaVista and Lexis/Nexis.

Undaunted, Page and Brin introduced Google, a search engine with some new and impressive technological twists, including broader, faster searches; within a remarkably short period of time, Google became the largest and most successful search engine on the Internet. Google attracted $25 million in venture funding from two Silicon Valley heavyweights, Sequoia Capital and Kleiner Perkins, and, eventually, after several years of solidifying its leadership position, filed an initial public offering in August 2004 that brought reminders of the Internet bubble. On the first day of trading, Google rang up a $27 billion market cap, making it larger than General Motors, and Page and Brin ended the day with a net worth near $4 billion each, at least on paper. More than 1,000 of the company's 2,300 employees were paper millionaires. All in all, not bad for a six-year-old startup.

UNDERSTANDING THE COMPETITIVE LANDSCAPE

However, the "build a better mousetrap" path to startup success may be more the exception than the rule. Our research revealed that defining and understanding the competitive landscape is a key factor for startups seeking funding and hoping for long-term success. While it would seem intuitive, many technology startups lose their way because the founding team gets fixated on product development and the intricacies of building a new company and neglects what may prove to be the most important question to be answered in a successful long-term plan: is there a market for the idea?

Our research revealed that while competitive position can be protected by patents or other types of temporary monopolistic barriers, the less successful companies, regardless of their technology innovation, perceived themselves to be in stronger competitive positions than they actually were.

In order to validate competitive position, startups must consider several factors:

- Cost structure

- Sales cycle

- Value proposition

- Patents on intellectual property

- Efficiency of manufacturing/sales processes

- Partnerships/channels
- Analysts/consultants response

Most technology startups provide incremental improvements to existing technologies, and the viability of their business plans lie in a carefully considered evaluation of the competition. Identifying and attacking small openings or market niches is often the path to value and sustainability.

In truth, at the heart of most startups is the founder's vision and interpretation of the market opportunity. This vision either flows smoothly into or runs up against customer expectations and marketplace realities. Often an entrepreneur's vision educates and *creates* the opportunity in the market. From Intel to Microsoft to Apple to Dell to Netscape, industry lore is filled with stories of visionaries who spawned markets with innovative technology and textbook execution. At the same time, there were thousands who anticipated markets, but failed to either find them or produce them. Thus competitive position is not necessarily simple to identify or quantify. The tension between an entrepreneur's concept and customers' perception creates more questions than answers for investors.

At some point competitive position must be validated in order to convince investors of the potential of a startup and the worthiness of an early-stage investment. This means not only demonstrating that the technology works but also that the above list of factors relating to competitive advantage are real.

Ron Bernal, a partner at Sutter Hill Ventures, a Silicon Valley venture capital firm, notes that finding entrepreneurs with intuitive skills about the competitive landscape and what customers really desire is one of the toughest tasks for startups to address. These strategists have the ability to listen to customers, synthesize exactly what they are seeking, and offer ways to position a startup's products.

"Startups are not the art of perfection, they are the art of trade-off," Bernal says. "Engineering can do almost anything with their technology and they will want to. But the question is how well are you listening to customers, beyond what they are saying, and distilling down, synthesizing, and driving an engineering plan with what you hear? Then you can figure out how to position yourself against competitors and how to insert your product into the market."

Having a CEO who understands these nuances is a tremendous advantage for a startup. It is why venture capitalists and other investors seek out founders and management teams with track records, with past successes in bringing a new venture to the marketplace. A key aspect of good leadership in a startup is the ability to critically think through exactly what it is that the company can demonstrate and how to demonstrate it to the marketplace. Often, startups run into problems because they simply are not demonstrating the right thing in the right way. A common VC refrain is: "You've demonstrated an interesting product, but you haven't demonstrated that anyone is going to pay for it."

JEFF TAYLOR

Founder and Chief Monster, Monster.com

Q: Monster.com has been an amazing success. What do you attribute it to?

Taylor: I come out of advertising, so I think about this a lot. But if you had to pick one single thing that made this company successful, just one, it would be our name. You can remember it. I read about some Web sites yesterday. I was sitting at the computer last night, but I couldn't remember the names of the Web sites I had read about. Our name— and the controversy that people associated with it at the beginning—is memorable.

Q: What was the controversy?

Taylor: People didn't like the name. But now, I think it's part of the vernacular. Monster equals jobs. Monster equals careers.

Q: It's become great branding.

Taylor: Yes. The name is perfectly likable today. I remember at the beginning my wife said to me that she wouldn't leave the house if I called the business Monster. It takes a certain amount of fortitude to say to your wife, "Well, hon, this is the name I'm going to use." And then my employees didn't like it either. And the clients didn't like it. So I basically had a barrage of negativity toward the idea of our name early on.

But today, Monster has been able to get to the point of being Kleenex or Band-Aid. It has become something of a generic term, like "go check out Monster." You could just as easily mean Careerbuilder or HotJobs, or something else. But doing a Monster search means looking for a job.

Something else, in terms of our early success, I have two friends, one that has four or five direct reports, and the other that's basically a sole proprietor. Neither of them likes having employees. I love having employees. I really love it. It inspires me. It motivates me. It's a big part of my passion, which is to help other people become successful. That spirit is a big part of the company.

Q: How does Monster make money?

Taylor: I developed the idea of a co-branded Web site for Ziff Davis. If you went to Ziff Davis, their career area was powered by Monster in 1996. I think we had a lot of firsts early on in those days, such as having a "powered by" Web site. We ended up with about eighty partnerships like that. We had one with Lycos and Excite and *USA Today*. Those partnerships were free. We brought the career center to the party and the partners provided the traffic.

We made money because it was traffic to our jobs, and we sold the jobs. That's our business model. Basically, 53 percent of our revenue comes from job postings. We sell job posting packages to companies. So a company like IBM might buy a 5,000 or an 8,000 job package, and then over time they might use all those up. Each job is actually for an area. You might buy a job for Boston, for Worcester, for Springfield, for Rhode Island, for Providence, that kind of thing. Fifty-three percent is jobs, and about 32–33 percent of our revenue comes from resumes. We have thirty-four million resumes in our resume database. Companies pay to get desktop access to that database. They can buy as small an area as Hoboken, New Jersey, and maybe five surrounding ZIP codes, or you can buy the whole country. You can buy it for a week or for the whole year.

Someone will buy the greater Chicago area for three months, and that will be a certain price. Then you get a user code, an X code, and then you can log in, and for three months use it, and then at the end of three months you get blocked.

Q: How many employees did you start with at Monster?

Taylor: I spun Monster out of Adion, the advertising agency I started. When I did, I took five people with me—the up-and-comers. I didn't take my lead people because I still needed them to run the agency. I took people that I thought had some promise and said to them, "Hey, you're going to work on this new project with me." The regret I have is that when I sold my ad agency and Monster, I never went back to get the great employees from the ad agency and bring them into the fold. Eventually all of them left. So even though they were in another part of the company, I couldn't keep them any longer. They were unhappy with me that I hadn't brought them along to Monster. It's taken me ten years to now get maybe a third of those employees to come back and work for me.

Q: TMP, a human resources recruiting and advertising agency, acquired Monster and changed its name to Monster.

Taylor: Yes. TMP Worldwide was renamed Monster Worldwide.

Q: And you've stayed in a role there the whole time, right?

Taylor: Yes. I've been president, CEO, chairman, and I'm now founder and Chief Monster. Most of the capacity I work in would be in strategy, marketing, and product development. I do a lot more of my work outside the company now. I've had an operational job running strategy and marketing products for the last two years.

Q: When did you leave the CEO role, and why?

Taylor: Basically, I was the CEO. When I started at TMP, I was the president of the Interactive Division. That division had one product, which was Monster. I knew it could be bigger than just Monster. Then I became CEO of TMP Interactive. Then when we merged TMP Worldwide and Monster and it became Monster Worldwide, my chairman, Andrew McKelvey, who was the founder, chairman, and CEO of TMP, said we can't have two founders, chairmen, CEOs. So he said, your title can be whatever you want, but it can't be CEO. Sometimes people called me the Chief Monster, so I was like, well, why don't I just be the Chief Monster, because I'm not hung up about it. I know the job I have to do.

Q: How would you characterize your leadership style?

Taylor: The thing about having employees is you have to have a lot of passion. I think that's a throwaway phrase because it's common knowledge that you need to be passionate. But some people are, and some people aren't. Some people are leaders and some people aren't. Some people will follow you to the ends of the earth. Other people won't. A lot has to do with the mission of the organization.

Now, I'm not very hung up at all about mission and vision and values and your core values and your objectives. I've never had a lot of religion around these headings. But I do believe in having something that you can believe in. I think the fact that we find millions of people jobs is not only relevant but it is something we can believe in. I say that because people are e-mailing us all day long, every day, saying, "I just found this job. My aunt just got a job on Monster. I saw a job on Monster for a job *at* Monster. I want to come and work at your company." People love this brand.

So, if you are somebody that enjoys having employees, then the next thing you have to have is a company product or mission or message or service that people really care about. I'm here because of that combination of loving to have employees and having a culture that basically respects employees, and is work hard, play hard. At every orientation, I say I have extremely high expectations, but I'm also extremely flexible.

My view is simple. For me, you're an adult. You do adult work here. I don't care what time you come to work or what time you go home. My first employees come to work around 4:30 in the morning. The last employees come to work about noon.

Q: Nobody has a problem with that?

Taylor: I think the managers have the hardest time. The employees don't have a hard time with that at all. It's always toughest to train managers in this environment, especially if they've been at companies with more rules.

Q: What advice do you give to people who want to start companies?

Taylor: I have a couple things that I've lived by, that I think are key to my own success. One of them—it's a Woody Allen quote—which is, "Eighty percent of success is showing up." I don't think it's just about success. I've kind of modified it. It's in my closet in a little square. Eighty percent of life is showing up. It isn't just about your successes. It's about all of your experiences. I really try to show up. The other thing is that we're taught, I think around the fourth grade, that the shortest distance between two points is a straight line. There is something so parochial and restricting about that. I've discovered that the shortest distance between two points is a big idea.

Q: When you look back, the period of time when Monster went from idea to creation to selling to TMP, how long are we talking about?

Taylor: A year.

Q: It was just one year?

Taylor: Yeah.

Q: Was selling it your exit strategy all along?

Taylor: I came up with the idea in December of '93, incorporated in April of '94. I entered into an agreement to be sold to TMP in April of '95 and sold it in November of '95. Basically, one month shy of two years from idea to selling the company. But I didn't sell Monster for very much money. I sold my ad agency at a fair premium and really gave Monster to TMP. I basically just about gave Monster to TMP with the idea that we'd start a new division.

Q: And what kept you from staying independent and building Monster on your own?

Taylor: There weren't really any Internet billionaires in 1995. That started happening in about 1998. There were only 200 Web sites when I started working with the Internet. Monster was about the 454th dot-com. It wasn't obvious that there were going to be thirty million Web sites, and that this was going to become as pervasive as it's become. For me, the other thing was that I had five or seven investors in my ad agency. They wanted me to keep working the ad agency. But I saw Monster as a much bigger idea. So TMP became an exit strategy, not just to find some liquidity for my investors but to find some real horsepower for me to be able to move into what I really thought was the big idea.

Q: You may not have become a billionaire, but you lasted, which is more than most dot-coms. Did you last because you teamed up with TMP?

Taylor: I think there were a couple reasons. One of our success factors is having a good business model. One of my experiences watching companies fall apart all around me was that if you don't have a good business model, you can't make up a business model. Either you have one that's inherent in your business, or you don't. And if you don't, you can't fake it.

WHO'S GOING TO PAY FOR IT?

When Charles Giancarlo joined the management team at Kalpana, for example, he had been part of several successful startups, as had other members of the team. One of the primary reasons he joined the struggling startup was that he recognized that the target market—Ethernet switching—was going to be a big market in the 1990s.

"It was the most predictable market in the world," Giancarlo says. "Part of the reason was that it was a technology that was replacing something that customers were already doing, i.e., Ethernet hubs, and it was clear that Ethernet was going to continue to grow. We were fairly experienced in that industry, so the paths to market were pretty clear." With a first-mover advantage, Kalpana quickly grabbed the lion's share of the nascent market and was then acquired by Cisco Systems.

For most startups, competitive position is determined not so much by the market opportunity but by the metrics one uses in validating one's own strengths and weaknesses going into the market.

Product differentiation is vital, but other key factors tend to play an even bigger role. For example, given similar product offerings, the startup with a more favorable and efficient cost structure has a distinct advantage with investors. Processes for producing the technology may be far superior. Targeting a specific market niche may afford a shorter, more efficient sales cycle. Monopolistic blocks such as patents may create daunting barriers to entry for competitors.

For investors, these factors can contribute either positively or negatively to competitive position. So the startup that can clearly validate its advantages will draw investors' interest. It is easy to boast about a better cost structure, but how do you prove it? An unbiased, third-party engineering study goes a long way to validating such claims, but savvy investors want to know who provided the study, what incentives that provider had—an early partnership with the startup, for example—to foster a certain outcome.

If a startup has already patented its technology, how good are those patents? Has there been a third-party patent review? Have the patents been issued yet? What is the prior art in that particular area? Are there any actions against the patent? Has the startup been able to license the technology to others? Has it been challenged in court? Did the startup win?

Thus our research showed that competitive position can be viewed in the abstract, the intellectual property aspect, or in hard and fast business data. Customers already validating a concept by beta testing a product and committing to an order are the most persuasive factors for investors. Getting results—and winning market share from competitors—is a compelling formula. And when competing against other startups, a well-connected sales force can make the difference. It is not uncommon for startups to recruit sales and marketing executives from key customers, which provides a significant competitive advantage when selling to that customer and that industry.

Investors inevitably want to know what will drive demand. Although predictions can be crapshoots, an informed investor is more likely to reap the rewards. Early investors in Google, for example, were aware of the crowded search engine marketplace. But Google provided something tangible: better results. Tests against others like Infoseek or AltaVista proved that Google always had better results. Searches yielded results in one page rather than two, and the cost of switching search engines was negligible. For busy users, faster, more comprehensive results were a tangible advantage, especially as the Web grew larger and larger over the years. It became increasingly clear that Google's technology model was superior. So even if it was the sixteenth or twenty-first player in the market, investors could map it clearly to determine its competitive position.

At the same time, online auctions seemed to be the wave of the future. With the stunning success of eBay, entrepreneurs rushed to create similar auction sites, and many investors poured money into the concept. The flaw was that people fundamentally misunderstood how some of these markets worked and what was important to customers. In some cases, the auction model led to the unbundling of services as part of the commodity offering. Though this might lead to cheaper services, the customer didn't want the hassle of separate purchases. This classic mismatch between expectations and reality is the cause of many startup failures.

TALK EARLY AND OFTEN WITH PROSPECTIVE CUSTOMERS

The most obvious method for avoiding this mismatch is to have active and open discussions with potential customers. Startups that keep everything under wraps in hopes of protecting innovation tend to hurt themselves more than help themselves. Talking to customers, getting a sense of their pain, the problems begging for solutions, and openly sharing product information is something startups ought to be doing. But many fear giving away trade secrets, and their stealth product development often leads to disappointment in the market.

During the Internet boom, some companies with sound business concepts failed because they did not take the time to understand their competitive position. Webvan, for example, an online grocery delivery startup with great potential, didn't take the time to prototype the concept, test it with customers, and validate the market and the value proposition. Thus a promising company flopped.

According to our research, less successful software companies focused quite early on what they perceived or hoped to be very large markets. As a result of what could have been a misperception, these companies never reached sufficient customer, revenue, or business model traction, and perhaps did not refocus quickly enough on smaller market niches where they might have been able to establish competitive barriers and possibly succeed.

Those who find the niches can create dramatic success stories. Jeff Taylor, the idiosyncratic founder of Monster.com, didn't only think outside the box, he dreamt outside it as well. While running his Boston-based advertising agency in 1994, he had a dream about creating a "monster" idea, an online bulletin board for job seekers. He awoke at 4:30 in the morning, dashed off to a local coffee shop, and designed the concept that eventually became Monster.com, the world's largest and most successful employment Web site, a name now synonymous with Help Wanted for those seeking jobs.

Among the reasons for Monster's success is one that is crucial for any startup: a clear and strategic understanding of competitive positioning in the marketplace. Entrepreneurs must do their homework and identify the entrenched players in a given market and figure out what their competitive advantage will be.

The high-tech highway is littered with casualties who believed themselves to be in stronger competitive positions than they actually were. Our research confirmed that startups with a clear picture of the marketplace and an ability to identify market niches in which they can compete and win are more likely to succeed.

In 1994, before the World Wide Web became a reality, Taylor foresaw Monster as a digital bulletin board. Though there were rumblings about the potential of the Internet as a communications and business tool, few were able to conceive of the sea change the Web would spawn in coming years. But Taylor already understood that his main competition was rooted in the old economy, the Help Wanted pages of local newspapers, and the recruiting firms or headhunters who focused on executive placement.

Taylor acknowledges that being first in a nascent media marketplace was important to his success. There were no Internet billionaires in 1994, and "most people thought I was off my rocker," he recalls. When he took his bulletin board concept online, it was still the early days, with only a few hundred Web sites and a handful of online businesses.

Taylor, an advertising veteran, believes that branding was the foundation for Monster's potent rise to success. The key to the company's survival and long-term success, he says, was rooted in building a brand. Taylor believes calling the company Monster.com was the single most important factor in staking out its competitive advantage in a crowded marketplace.

"I can't remember the names of any of the Web sites I visited last night or last week," Taylor says. "But people had a stronger reaction to this than they would for other names. I could have called it Careerbuilder.com or HotJobs or something else. But Monster has become a Kleenex or Band-Aid, a generic term for looking for a job."

ATTACK FROM BELOW

For startups that don't have first-mover advantage, entering an available market niche and slowly spreading into larger, higher end markets can be just as powerful. Dell Computer began in Michael Dell's dorm room with the idea of selling cheap personal computers built with commodity parts. By grabbing the low end of the market at the outset and building an innovative supply chain, Dell eventually penetrated all levels of the PC market and became the dominant player.

The attack from below strategy gives a startup an opportunity to find market niches and avoid going head to head in premium markets with established players. And while conventional wisdom suggests that startups that are first into new market spaces have an advantage, that is not always the case.

Yuchun Lee of Unica Software was clear from the outset that he had no intention of being the pioneer with arrows pointed at his back. By carefully scouting the enterprise software sector Lee concluded that the first wave of players into the market have the most difficult time. They must spend time and resources educating the market about the new capabilities of the software, a process that can take years.

"Our strategy is to focus on markets that already have taken shape and go in and compete and beat out the first wave," Lee says. "You know the mistakes they made, the market is now more educated, and there's more feedback for the next wave. So we focus on building a leapfrog product to go out into the market."

In certain industry segments, competitive position is more

complex to secure. In the biotechnology sector, startups must court the pharmaceutical giants with a viable and alluring idea. "You have to be able to tell your story to the pharmaceutical industry," says Mark Levin, founder and CEO of Millennium Pharmaceuticals in Cambridge, Massachusetts. "Early on, if you can't go out and convince the pharmaceutical industry that you've got the right people, the right vision, the right story, and the right set of goals, you won't be successful."

Millennium was founded in 1993, at the height of the fervor over the sequencing of the human genome. The excitement surrounding the genomic revolution gripped the venture capital market as tightly as the Internet would a few years later. Timing was everything, Levin points out. He recalls that six months after the official founding of Millennium, whose stated goal was to develop products from genomics research, he was scheduled to speak to a venture capital conference in California. Right before he was set to go on, the director of research and development for Roche, the Swiss pharmaceuticals giant, was speaking. When he got to his last slide, he said to the audience, "Next, I'm going to tell you what the future of the entire pharmaceuticals industry is." Levin was frozen in his seat wondering what he was going to hear. "He put up his last slide and it had one word: genomics," Levin says. "I said, 'Thank goodness.'" Within two months, Levin had made an important deal with Roche.

Our research confirmed that startups, no matter how meticulously they scope out competitive position, are often at the mercy of forces beyond their control. In most specialized technology markets, like software and services, the competitive landscape is often shaped to a large degree by the leading industry analysts, the technology media, and the large vendors such as Microsoft, IBM, or Hewlett-Packard. John Landry, the veteran investor and entrepreneur, points out that the road to success lies in the establishment of strong relationships with these leading influencers.

"You have to get to the analysts," Landry says. "You have to court them because you want to get mentioned in the newsletters and reports. In the early stage of an industry, like mobile applications, for example, the analysts don't want to go out on a limb, so you get lumped in with twelve other companies. The list gets smaller as the industry matures. And by building relationships with the analysts, it gives buyers—IT executives, in particular—the idea that this is a company we can do business with because they are being followed by the analysts."

Getting mentioned by the industry press, or having an opportunity to demonstrate a product at industry events like Demo, often leads to important endorsements. And perhaps the most important connection is with giants like Microsoft as it is preparing a new release of a major product suite such as Windows.

Like pilot fish on a whale, startups can ride these strategic relationships to successful results. "By infiltrating your way into Microsoft's new environment, given that they can't do everything, they want to have companies with them that are going to showcase how they've used these new Microsoft technologies to build their new products," Landry says. "You then become part of their marketing. And the dollars used to roll out these products will be huge."

To summarize, there is no single path to successful competitive positioning. But startups lower the odds significantly by:

- Spending whatever time is necessary to identify the market, talk to potential customers, share their concepts and ideas, and create not only customers but advocates.

- Focusing on cost structure, sales processes, marketing, manufacturing processes, partnerships, and industry analysts to create competitive advantage.

- Stressing not only product development but identifying an audience that is willing to buy the product.

- Validating the market in a variety of ways in order to persuade investors that the value proposition is real and potent.

As we will see in the next chapter, identifying the competitive position is merely a crucial first step. Putting in place a strong and strategic business model is essential for building a path to value.

"You can have the right idea," says Cisco's Giancarlo, "but if you can't execute on it—and not just getting the product to work but then getting to the marketplace properly—you won't have anything."

What entrepreneurs learn, sometimes painfully, is that scoping out the market size and figuring out competitive position are key. But as we shall see in the next chapter, the business model serves as the blueprint for a startup's strategy. A strong business model attracts investors and increases valuations in succeeding rounds of financing.

———

## Eight

Business Models: It's Not Just What You Do, It's How You Do It

One of the most important yet least intuitive factors in building a successful startup is the creation of a rigorous and functional business model. Most of the legendary startup success stories, such as Dell Computer, Staples, Federal Express, Home Depot, and Monster.com, were built upon business models that fundamentally altered the industry in which they competed.

Our research showed that how a company is organized to do business matters a lot, perhaps more than any other axis point. In fact, we followed up a year after our initial research with a study group to determine how our research companies had progressed. We created an additional set of Star Charts to compare the characteristics of the companies that successfully completed another round of funding with those companies that did not. What we found was that *the business model is the key factor that leads to success in early stage companies.* Business model and product development clearly are the key determinants for obtaining additional funding rounds. In addition, the business model, combined with accurately estimating the right market size, is crucial to companies strengthening their business position and improving their chances for acquisition, merger, and profitability.

These findings were not a surprise. One common characteristic of startups is the uncertainty about the future. What an entrepreneur and his team expect to happen often doesn't happen or it happens far differently than anticipated. Thus the business model becomes not only a design for doing business but a compass point for growth and expansion. There's a certain Zen-like feel to the idea of moving moment to moment, knowing that by focusing on the right metrics you can *create* the possibilities as you bring in those possibilities.

Unfortunately, "business model" is a term that is shrouded in ambiguity. It can be abused and misunderstood in the discussion about startups. Often, the concept of a business model is confused with market strategy, which helps, at least in part, explain the boom and bust nature of the high-tech sector in recent years.

DEFINING OUR TERMS

For our purposes, we view market strategy as a focus on which customer a company is addressing and how it is delivering value to that customer. What is the market? Who is the primary customer? What are the customer's needs? What is the value proposition for the customer's business?

The business model, on the other hand, focuses on how a startup captures some of that value for itself. *The business model determines the viability of a company.* It focuses on the coordination of business processes, both internally and externally, determining how a startup interacts with its solution partners, channel alliances, and customers. But it is mostly an inward-facing equation that requires self-awareness, insight, and facile analysis by the entrepreneur and his or her team (with critical investor help as well).

CHARLES GIANCARLO

Senior Vice President and General Manager
of Product Development, Cisco Systems

Q: At Cisco, where you've acquired hundreds of companies and integrated them into your business, how do you define success?

Giancarlo: You really do need to define it. Sometimes we look at a company and might say, well, that's a great technology, but it's not really a product. Or we may say, that's a great product and it's not really a company. So there are various levels of success. You could sell something that's a pure technology—and when I say, "sell it," I mean sell the company to a potential buyer. In which case, it might be deemed to be a success from the vantage point of the investors and of the employees, but certainly not from the standpoint of somebody who looks at companies and certainly not from the point of view of investors who wanted to take the company public.

So there are many definitions. I say that because we buy technology companies all the time. We recently bought a company called Twingo, which was really two guys with some technology that was of interest to us. We mainly wanted the two guys, but we had to buy it all together. There are companies that we buy that have products that for one set of reasons or another were never able to create a company around those products. And yet those products may be of interest to us and so our interest in the company is to make it successful.

Q: Cisco has always been famous for buying people, so to speak. That is, buying startups that are in their early stages—sometimes without products—but with good people and with promise. Is that still the case?

Giancarlo: Yes. We still like to buy great teams.

Q: In our study, we found that often the management team is more important than the technology. Have you found that to be the case?

Giancarlo: I would tend to agree with that, with the following caveat, which is to say that if the management piece is really good, you would expect the technology piece would be pretty good. As a result, from the standpoint of an acquisition, having a really good management team is one of Cisco's prerequisites for buying the company out. If there's not a strong management team there, then the company and the success of that company will probably not survive acquisition.

Q: You were part of a startup, Kalpana, that was acquired by Cisco. Was your objective from the outset to be acquired?

Giancarlo: Actually, Kalpana certainly had the option of going public, and for a set of reasons that I'll go into, the company decided to be sold instead. Kalpana was started by two guys, and it was originally seed-funded by an angel investor, as well as by a well-known venture capital firm. The idea was Ethernet switching.

Not too long after it was started, the company got into a little trouble. They had developed the product, but it was not really finished, and it didn't work properly. At that point, the company was effectively in a bit of a crisis and had been restarted. So a new CEO came in. Actually, the angel came in as CEO. Basically he let go the entire senior management team and two-thirds of the employees, with the exception of the two original founders. So the two original founders were there, and no other management team, other than the CEO. That's when I went there.

Q: What lured you there in the aftermath of such a big management shakeout?

Giancarlo: Well, everyone understood that Ethernet switching was going to be a big market. It was the most predictable market in the world, in my view. And part of the reason for that was that it was a technology that was replacing something that customers were already doing— using Ethernet hubs. So it was very clear to me that Ethernet was going to continue to grow and that Kalpana really had a better way of doing something that the market was already doing. As a result, it seemed to me that the company could grow rapidly.

What the new CEO did was bring in a new management team. Then he dealt with the problems which were related to both engineering and manufacturing. The next thing he did was to create a new product roadmap. We had to do that because by the time they had finished fixing the product, a number of other companies were beginning to focus on the market. Next he was able to bring in new financing for the company. With all those things done, it really felt like we could make this company a very strong leader.

Q: What you are illustrating is what a strong management team can do, which is to say, turn a failing startup into a successful one.

Giancarlo: Absolutely. Six months after the new CEO was in place, the company really started to perform extremely well and growth was very good. Then when the management team went in front of the board, it was pretty much all good news. We had formed partnerships with Sun, with HP, with IBM, and it was at that time that the CEO started to discuss with IBM the possibility of IBM buying out Kalpana. IBM expressed interest in it. Then we started a very lengthy process of due diligence with IBM, and it stretched on for months and months and months. Finally, IBM put an offer on the table, and pretty much just as they did that, maybe just a little bit after they had done that, Cisco came up with an unsolicited offer for Kalpana. They were very serious about it and pressed it pretty hard. One of the key things here was that the CEO did not want to go to IBM. But IBM made it a condition of its offer. Cisco did not make it a condition of its offer and we tilted in their direction. This, of course, is ironic because John Chambers, Cisco's chairman and CEO, said to me that keeping a management team in place was the key to the successful acquisition. So in this case, he was willing to go against the grain.

To create a business model, a startup must first figure out what business it is in. This may sound simple, but the number of start-ups that fail because they were unable to define themselves within a specific industry is astronomical. Richard Branson built Virgin Atlantic Airways into a stunning success because he knew from the outset that he could not compete head-on with giants like British Airways and American Airlines. They were in the transportation business. But Virgin would look at it differently. When you put hundreds of people inside a large metal tube and fly them for several hours from one city to another, the happiest customers and the ones most likely to return are the ones who have the best experience. So Branson decided Virgin was in the *entertainment* business, not the transportation business, and proceeded to incorporate seatback videos, playful flight attendants, better food, and fun accoutrements such as flying pajamas and free headsets into the Virgin experience.

The business model therefore is about defining organizational strategy and business processes. In a sense, customers should be agnostic about the business model. The business model is not their concern. Shareholders, on the other hand, should be deeply interested in a business model because it will make the difference between success and failure. It will do nothing less than determine if you make money. An entrepreneur must consider his or her great idea and put it in the context of a single question: How will I deliver this value proposition to the customer? By delivering it this way, can I generate revenues and profits? What is clear from our research is that a startup might identify customers with unmet needs, determine a value proposition, and still fail because it didn't get the business model right.

THE PRICING MODEL

The business model also measures a company's ability to articulate a pricing model that will eventually take advantage of positive economies of scale. In order to build value over time, a startup must create a viable pricing model, and within that model a framework for a sales cycle that offers the best advantage in building and sustaining revenues. A strong business model provides the structure for building a company from scratch with the type of discipline and focus that become the foundation for success. It can also offer the type of differentiation that fuels significant competitive advantage.

For example, Captivate Networks, a startup that supplies wireless content for video screens in elevators, used a clever market strategy to position itself as a media provider rather than a technology company. In so doing, it devised a pricing model similar to print and broadcast media outlets, selling advertising packages to big corporate accounts that pay by the number of eyeballs Captivate can generate.

But Captivate took it a step further. In order to secure the content, it approached the content providers such as the *New York Times* and CNN and said, "We'd like to put your programming on our screens." According to Michael DiFranza, founder and CEO, the response was positive until the content providers asked how much Captivate was willing to pay. "We said, we're not willing to pay anything," DiFranza explains. "If you provide us with your programming, we'll be happy to expose your brand to our viewers because our viewers are coming whether I put a test pattern up on that screen or your content."

Captivate not only forged strong relationships with forty different programming partners but eventually got them to pay for the exposure. "We flipped it around on them," DiFranza says of the business model, which eventually led to Captivate's acquisition by Gannett.

But pricing is just a part of the business model formula. Figuring out how to sell what you make is a broader, more complex undertaking. The business model will affect not only who your customers are but also business partners, channels, alliances, and the very culture of those organizations. Those who devise innovative and practical business models have far greater chances of long-term success.

Large, traditional organizations have structure and momentum in the functioning of the business. Business processes implemented long ago and deeply engrained in the organization move forward under their own weight. Things persist because of this momentum. But within startups there is hardly any structure at all. In fact, most of what a startup is doing is creating structure on the fly. The feeling is akin to a wave form. What a CEO of a startup is trying to do is get that wave form stable. Yet how does a leader create a pattern or shape to something? How do you know what to focus on when you must focus on everything?

Successful startups find a way to get their arms around the chaos, often with investor or VC help, by creating a business model with what we call *rigorous flexibility*. In this there is just enough discipline to keep the chaos from undermining the nascent efforts, but enough malleability to allow for quick starts and stops and changes in direction.

WHAT WE FOUND

What we found in our research:

- The business model axis measured whether or not companies had demonstrated an ability to sell at economies of scale. Successful startups had developed pricing models and demonstrated economies of scale leading to profitability. A startup must be able to grow the business quickly as customer acceptance spreads and demand increases.

- Successful startups demonstrated business models that were sustainable. If a startup is unable to sustain early success, competitors will step in and take away the market.

- The successful startups developed models that allowed them to remain quick and nimble. Shorter sales cycles are better. There is truth to the high-tech notion that you are either quick or dead.

- In the R&D-intensive industries such as telecommunications and semiconductors, the successful companies in this category began life with a more developed business model than the less successful firms, perhaps indicating a better early understanding of the economic value of their products.

- The most successful software companies paid more attention than their less successful counterparts to growing revenue and building a scalable business model.

- While most dot-coms that survived the bubble acquired respectable customer bases, few made significant progress on their business models, indicating a lack among them of pricing models that could have led to increased growth and profitability.

Knowing all this is one thing; executing on it is another. One of our clear findings in the search for paths to value is how difficult the business model is to build and how elusive it becomes in an environment that is generally chaotic and confusing. High-tech entrepreneurs may be visionary when it comes to technology, but are often sadly lacking in the ability to create a business model that will make their business scalable, sustainable, and fleet of foot.

Engineering entrepreneurs always seek a template, a tried and true solution to the problem. Yet just as there is no single path to value, there is no single method for achieving sound business model creation. If anything, a business model evolves with careful nurturing over an extended period of time. It requires introspection and collaboration, trial and error, fitting and retrofitting.

The enlightened entrepreneur, like Yuchun Lee of Unica, is a student of business trends as well as a technologist. He spent countless hours studying and benchmarking the potential competition before launching Unica. As an entrepreneur and a pragmatist, he was unusual among founders of technology startups. He specifically positioned Unica to be in the second wave in the enterprise marketing software space in order to avoid the costly and time-consuming role of pioneer.

Lee spent most of his time honing the business model and learned some valuable lessons. "If your single objective is just to bring in revenue, that's one type of business," he says. "But if your objective is to build a successful company, that's another type of business. Being able to manage cash while you grow has to be part and parcel of your business model. Otherwise, the model will not be fine tuned to generate cash and be profitable. How can a company that doesn't factor that in expect to suddenly grow up and become profitable?"

BENCHMARKING

By benchmarking Unica against other companies when they were at Unica's size, Lee was able to get a clear sense of expense levels for different parts of the venture, including key areas such as R&D and GNA. "It's a comfort to know that I'm not reinventing the wheel, that plenty of other successful companies have done it and I'm just using the guideline they put in place," Lee says. "We factor in those guidelines along with the size of the markets we'll go after to make sure they are big enough to sustain this type of business."

In a crowded technology marketplace, benchmarking may be useful, but not necessarily enough. For example, a software startup considering its business model needs to ask: Am I delivering a product or a service? Do I create a business model like a Software.com or Siebel Systems? Software.com is a service provider, Siebel a software vendor. Both offer similar features and functions, but in very different delivery mechanisms. A startup must decide which path will better lead to sales and profits.

When IBM opened up its WebSphere platform to create a community of third-party developers, it made the decision that it would not be able to bring applications quickly enough to the market itself. In order to ramp-up market acceptance of this enterprise e-business on demand software platform and achieve scalability more quickly, it made a business model decision to allow partners to join the rollout. In essence, IBM said, "We believe this legion of third parties will find the sweet spot faster than our own engineers in house."

In the 1980s, Digital Equipment Corporation chose the opposite business model and kept its software proprietary, believing that it had the best solution and understood what its customers needed and wanted better than the customers did. It was a costly mistake, leading to the demise of the giant computer maker, which was eventually absorbed by Compaq and then Hewlett-Packard.

Microsoft chose another business model: bundling its software offerings to drive its empire. Though competitors consistently offered superior technology, Microsoft's business model effectively provided a monopoly that fueled fast and overwhelming growth.

The path to value over the long term is marked by an evolution—not just building one successful product but having a vision about a product line, a product extension that provides a passageway to the future. It is not just a market entry business model for getting the first few customers but also a scalable business model that will be the foundation for growth.

For example, Google did not invent the search engine marketplace, but by taking its time going public, the startup was able to build better technology and evolve a business model that dominates its market space. It wasn't necessarily the business model Google would have gone public with if it had jumped on the IPO bandwagon three or four years earlier. By taking its time, the company was able to focus more on a business model that it could scale up in the *right* way.

SHIFTING MODELS

During the Internet bubble, time frames were accelerated to what proved to be untenable levels, leaving startups little time to develop and hone strong business models. Most failed. Many that survived what was perhaps the most sweeping reversal in venture capital history have revamped their business models completely, taking the online model and shifting it to a software provider model. In order to make that shift, these companies had to revisit every facet of how to build and deliver their products.

Business models undoubtedly shift as a startup grows. Lotus Development Corporation began in the early 1980s selling an off-the-shelf spreadsheet package, Lotus 1-2-3; but over time, as the marketplace changed, Lotus moved its focus from packaged software to Notes, the enterprise-wide collaboration groupware, which dictated a complete remaking of its business model. Suddenly the company had to target corporate IT customers, sell licenses in various iterations, and hire a direct sales force. Ultimately the business model could not be sustained and Lotus was acquired by IBM.

Pricing models can shift dramatically for software companies depending on whether a startup is going it alone or selling through an integrator who resells the software as part of a package. Often, startups are forced to offer lower prices to appease skeptical customers who worry about doing business with a brand-new player. Why should I pay premium prices to a company that might not be here in five years, the customer will ask?

Venture capitalists, who expect to see positive growth and movement in their investments, can apply pressure to startups to increase revenues quickly. They also are loath to leave money on the table if startups lower prices to win business. The pressure to find a viable pricing model, therefore, becomes intense.

High-tech entrepreneurs may well be the worst group from which to seek business model wisdom. They tend to be focused on the technology and lack the business acumen to shape a viable business model. Some analysts who track the Silicon Valley attribute the boom-and-bust cycles of the technology sector to this dearth of business model expertise.

"One of the biggest challenges facing an entrepreneur is to acknowledge the limits of his competence," says consultant Amiel Kornel, who has worked closely with many startups. "Most want to believe they can do it all. The successful ones have a keen sense of where their strengths lie and where they need to rely on others."

Entrepreneurs with successful track records are magnets for capital and talent. They are able to hire a management team who knows how to build and innovate successful business models. For those who haven't achieved such proof points, the alternative is to turn to the venture capitalists and consultants who specialize in building business models.

Often, early-stage startups will turn to local business schools with programs designed to provide research and analysis. They may hire newly minted MBAs to bring a business focus. But eventually a successful startup must have the expertise on the management team in order to succeed.

FINDING THE OBJECTIVE

Martin Coyne, the former Kodak executive who sits on the board at Akamai, says that he has learned over the course of his career to always begin his due diligence with a fundamental question about the business model: What is your objective? What do you want to achieve? "If you don't know what you want to achieve, you are all over the place," Coyne says. "Everything ought to be measured against your objective."

One of the obvious objectives is to generate cash. Most startups fail simply because they burn through their cash faster than they can ramp-up revenues. This is where a strong business model helps. If a company can generate cash, it can ride through weak periods due to the economy or the marketplace.

Successful startups, presumably ensconced in a market space in which they can grow, carefully manage the sales and growth process. By working within a business plan that is designed to control and forecast growth, a startup with a strong culture of internal accountability will not only survive but thrive.

At Unica, for example, Lee instituted a process called Top Five. Every individual in the company has a set of five goals against which he or she is measured every year. The expectation is universal. You've got to hit the goal you set for yourself or you let the company down. For a salesperson, a Top Five goal might be to generate a 98 percent renewal rate from the company's maintenance base. For a developer, if Unica is entering a new market and is targeting revenue in that market at X millions of dollars, a Top Five goal might include reducing the postintegrated test bug count by 10 percent or 20 percent. Internally, everyone is measured against the Top Five goals.

"Imagine if the entire company's commitment is based on these numbers and metrics," Lee says. "We're rolling up the planning process to figure out how much investment we want and this won't let the company invest too far ahead. It's a self-check."

Unfortunately few early-stage startups have the internal discipline and wisdom to initiate such concepts. The luxury of such analytical thinking does not come until later financing rounds when the company is preparing to leave survival mode.

In order to get to these later rounds, we've concluded that the business model is the key factor that leads to success in early-stage companies. Business model and product development are the key determinants for obtaining additional funding rounds. And as we shall see in the next chapter, product development, especially in marketplaces teeming with competitors, is the next great challenge for an entrepreneur.

## Nine

Product Development: You've Got to Have Something "Cool" to Sell

The last axis focuses on performance. Within that domain are product development, customer acquisition, and alliances/distribution channels. Early-stage investors and management teams of startups need to ask themselves hard questions about these three metrics: When should I invest more in further developing my product? How and when should I engage channels? What level of customer traction justifies investment in ramping up sales? Is a more developed product better in the early stages? To answer these and other questions, we start with product development.

At the heart of most high-tech startups is a passionate visionary with the seed of an idea. Most entrepreneurs are technologists driven by the quest for the next new thing—and to make money on the resulting product.

But product development is not just about the product: it is also about process, about customer involvement and input, about channels and partnerships, and about when to invest and how much to invest in research and development. In short, it is about execution across multiple disciplines.

Whether the idea emerges as a product or service, the entrepreneur must decide the best route to take the idea from concept to reality. But as our research showed, that path can be a confusing and chaotic one, lined with unexpected obstacles and crucial decisions that must be made correctly in order to attain success. For every product that achieved greatness, be it the Palm Pilot, Apple Macintosh, Amazon.com, or Norton Anti-Virus software, there are legions that fell by the wayside, lost in poorly executed product development efforts.

For successful startups, product development cannot be done in a vacuum. Entrepreneurs and their fledgling management teams must decide when and how to tie product development together with customer acquisition and a sound business model. In other words, startups need to get to customers as soon as possible, sharing concepts, exploring product options, listening to customers' needs, and testing concepts in real-world settings.

EARLY CUSTOMER INPUT

Martin Coyne, lead director at Akamai, brings both a large-company and startup perspective to the table. Coyne was executive vice president at Kodak and led the company's efforts into the world of digital photography. He says there is no substitute for early customer input into product development. From the entry generation, those innovators and early adopters who articulate a need, to later customers, the technology must reflect experiences and changes that customers encounter in their own work settings.

"While it all looks crystal clear at the beginning, as customers use a product, you gain insight," Coyne says. "You make iterative improvements in the base products that reflect changes in behavior, changes in work flow, and other external changes. After a year or two of iterative improvements, you end up with the big revenue opportunity for the next generation."

The Paths to Value research showed, not surprisingly, that the most successful companies paid more attention than their less successful counterparts to growing revenue and to building a scalable business model. These companies also made greater and steadier progress on the product development value axis. The research also showed that service-intensive companies rely much less on physical capital or manufacturing and have shorter product development life cycles, while software companies made greater and steadier progress on product development.

But there was also a more surprising finding: *a more developed product is not always better.* A large number of the failed software companies achieved significant product development as they burned through investment dollars without achieving robust progress in customer acquisition and cash flow. Thus getting ahead of yourself in product development to the exclusion of other complementary metrics can lead to disaster.

Our research revealed that less successful companies started out with better initial product development—perhaps indicating premature levels of commitment to one type of product or what is commonly referred to as a technology-driven approach as opposed to a customer- or market-driven approach. Successful companies started slowly, but accelerated at a steady pace.

In the telecommunication and semiconductor sectors, for example, *less* successful firms raised their seed financing at higher valuations and *emphasized well-developed products* and strong early competitive positions. At initial financing, these companies were farther along than successful companies on the product development axis and perceived themselves to be in stronger initial competitive positions. By later financing rounds, however, the more successful companies had moved ahead of their less successful counterparts on most measurements.

In fact, at any given stage of financing, successful R&D-intensive firms focused *less* on product development than successful service-intensive firms. This finding confirmed an initial hypothesis that capital-intensive manufacturers took longer than their service-intensive companies to move from alpha to beta, to working versions of their products.

Surprisingly for R&D-intensive firms in the telecommunications and semiconductor sectors, a high score on the product development axis did not always indicate success. Rather, on average, successful companies showed steady growth along this axis in conjuction with progress on the customer acquisition value axis. The scores of less successful companies were higher early on, but did not increase much over time. Such a finding often indicates R&D restarts and suggests that some technology-driven ventures get ahead of themselves with respect to customer and market validation.

When we surveyed respondents later on, during late 2003, our earlier conclusions were confirmed. Investors are swayed by two factors: business model and product development. Both are clearly the key determinants for obtaining additional funding rounds. Overestimating market size and poor product development stand out as key factors in the failure of early-stage companies to obtain additional venture funding.

MICHAEL DIFRANZA

Founder, President, and General Manager,
Captive Networks

Q: Captivate Networks puts screens in elevators so you can see and read news and see stock quotes. How did you come up with the idea?

DiFranza: It was around the time of PointCast. That was a product that was essentially a news-based screen saver. It put news and stock quotes on your computer screen at work. It was a great idea. But it was always clogging up everybody's data network. As soon as you'd download PointCast, the IT guys in most companies would shut it off.

What's interesting is that around that time, I spent each flight going back and forth to Oregon, writing down ideas for companies I would like to start. I had just gone through a program at Harvard and I really felt I was ready to slay a bigger dragon than at Mentor. On every flight out to Oregon I'd write down a list of ideas for companies. On every flight back to Boston I'd cross out the ideas because they were just bad ideas or they had issues. So I already had the mindset that I wanted to go off and do something. That's when the idea behind Captivate hit me.

Q: What did you do next?

DiFranza: When I sat down and really started to think about the business, and started to think about how to do it, I realized no one's ever done it before. I mean, there were a lot of unknowns. When we sat down and really started to take a look at who the different constituencies were for the service, we found there were a lot of them. You had the viewer, first and foremost, because everything centers around the viewer. You had the real estate guys that essentially gave you access and allowed you to build your distribution. You had the elevator guys that actually had to install these systems in their elevators. You had the programming and content partners, because we didn't want to put a big new staff together. And then we had the advertisers. We had to figure out our value proposition for each of those constituencies.

Q: How much of your success was timing?

DiFranza: Partly. At the same time when we were rolling out our company, there seemed to be a huge consolidation going on in the real estate industry under real estate investment trusts, where a single company like Equity Office Properties, Boston Properties, or Trizec were rolling up a lot of buildings. A lot of these companies were also trying to establish their brand. What does it mean to be in an Equity Office building? What does it mean to be in a Trizec building? Why do you care as a consumer?

So we saw that they had a branding need and we said, "How do we configure this system so that the real estate developers can brand themselves as part of our execution?" One of the products that we developed and patented was something called Screen Center, which allows building managers to publish information to the screens. We could even have real estate marketing departments put branding messages up on our screens across the entire portfolio while having the local building manager communicating with tenants about local events, like fire alarm tests.

The other thing that we recognized was that real estate guys are money driven. As a result, we recognized that we had to create a revenue opportunity for them to participate in. So we created a tenant amenity for them. We created a communication tool for them. We let them share in the advertising revenue. In other words, we created a new revenue stream for them that did not exist prior to Captivate's invention. We created wins for them. And we also addressed some of the business problems they had.

Q: How important was technology?

DiFranza: As I mentioned, I came out of Mentor Graphics. The founders of Mentor did not just focus on technology—features and functions. They focused on how technology creates value for business. The idea was that if you solve a problem for someone, there will always be money. That's how I look at technology.

Q: How did that translate in practice?

DiFranza: One of the decisions that we had to make was that the screens needed to communicate with the server that is connected to the Internet. Your choices were to hang a traveling cable down the elevator shaft to connect the screen to the server or a switch. Very expensive. Very time consuming, because you're talking about big cables. Consider a 100-story building. You're talking about bringing in a forklift with a giant wheel of wire on it. It's very expensive. In 1997, we implemented the system via wireless technology.

Q: For wireless, that was very early.

DiFranza: We were bleeding edge. Bleeding. We were one of Cisco's largest WiFi customers in the early days, because we were out there. And we needed to do that because that allowed us to scale very rapidly. At our peak we were installing 400 elevators a month. We went from essentially no audience to an audience of one million-plus people in something like an eighteen-month window.

Even with WiFi, our technology costs were expensive. In the early days, you had technology, and then you had labor. And labor—because an elevator is a safety system— you needed to be able to go in and have a qualified mechanic do the work. And so we used union labor. It was very expensive. Our initial systems were in the $12,000 to $15,000 per unit range. That's big money. A big investment.

We raised money through venture capital and also through funding that the real estate guys actually provided us. So we got our customers to become partners in the business.

Q: How have you protected yourself against competition?

DiFranza: We were first. We have a lot of market share—75 percent. We also have a lot of patents. Since I came out of the technology world, I understand the value of patents, and we are very aggressive in patenting our technology. That makes it extremely difficult, if not impossible, for somebody to do this without infringing on our technology.

———

WHAT THEY NEED

Venture capitalists, early customers, and prospective channel partners require *proof points* from a startup in order to feel comfortable making a commitment. Product development is a key proof point. In order to garner early-stage traction with these key stakeholders, a startup must be able to demonstrate that it cannot only build the product—get it to work reliably and get it out the door in a reasonable time frame—but also that it has a product road map for future development.

From the first demonstration to the first ship date, startups find themselves under intense pressure, which is why it is no surprise that so many fail. Once an initial investment is made, the clock starts ticking. Investors and prospective customers don't want to hear "Let it age like a fine wine. Don't rush it." In a high-tech windstorm of change, speed matters, scalability matters, sustainability matters.

Since the Internet bubble, product development tools, particularly in the software arena, have improved dramatically, which has resulted in far shorter product development cycles. In the software and services sectors, two-year development cycles are a thing of the past, and startups find themselves in pitched battles to get products out faster and more cheaply with better results. Companies, without the luxury of free capital and extended windows of opportunity, must get products right the first time. Recovering from early-stage missteps is difficult, and the risk of losing early cornerstone customers can damage or destroy a startup's chances for survival.

Ironically, far too many entrepreneurs hamstring their own efforts by neglecting to take advantage of the most fertile research ground for new products: the customers themselves.

Too many startups place themselves in "stealth mode" during product development cycles and refuse to share their concepts with customers for fear of having their ideas stolen. This, our research showed, is a formula for failure. The high-tech superhighway is littered with wrecks that were once someone's passionate idea but became casualties of shoddy execution and misplaced focus. Entrepreneurs who mine the needs and wisdom of customers, channel partners, and industry analysts can usually find out everything they need to know about driving product development. There is no substitute for good, open conversation and the ability to listen, really listen, to a customer's anguish. Solve a customer's problem and the money will follow.

"In early stages of a startup, you have to have a terrific focus on customer products," says Alex Osadzinski, a venture capitalist. "And customers will tell you for free whether they will buy your products or not. You never get false negatives. If the customer says, 'I don't want to buy that,' they never do."

Osadzinski adds that he is amazed how often he sees early-stage companies with great products who've not shown them or discussed them with prospective customers. "They say they are not quite ready," Osadzinski says. "They say they can't get a meeting with the target customer. So I ask, How is it you are planning to sell this? If you can't figure out how to get to those folks and say, 'Here is the product, what do you think?' before you sell to them, they are sure as hell not going to tell you anything after you've produced the product."

Unfortunately far too many startups lose sight of the end goal and neglect customer input. For companies that allow product development to proceed well ahead of marketplace input, there is significant danger. Yet entrepreneurs—even if they acknowledge this aspect of the development cycle—are often at a loss in their ability to analyze customer responses. Are customers telling me the truth? Are they simply fantasizing about what they would like to have or is this a product they will actually buy? Is the person I'm speaking to actually going to make the buying decisions?

Coyne says it is not enough to have just the technical people out in the field talking to customers. A startup needs its senior management team out there as well, sitting down and trying to understand where they are and where customers and partners are going with the product.

In other words, everyone should be part of the product development effort.

HOW TO GET THERE

While many factors contribute to successful product development, four stood out:

- *Product development must be market focused.* Too many technology-driven startups fail to create harmony between product development and customer acquisition. But to succeed, a startup must have both.

- *Prioritization is key.* Startups must ask a series of key questions about the product early in the development cycle in order to find a feature set that can be quickly demonstrated and offered to customers. One strong product feature that can lead to customer traction is worth far more than five features that take longer and cost more to develop.

- *Product development cannot be linear.* Startups must extrapolate product development out into the future, making the difficult but necessary decisions about where the technology is going to be.

- *Cash flow is king.* Startups need to demonstrate revenue generation quickly because there is little investor money available in later financing rounds if there is no revenue. Therefore, successful startups find the delicate balance between honing a product and taking it out to the marketplace quickly.

As with everything else in life, nothing is as straightforward and simple as surveys and polls would indicate. For startups, paths to value diverge all over the map depending on the end goal and exit strategy of the founders. Many startups, in the telecommunications sector, for example, view success as the ability to be acquired quickly by a bigger player. Industry giants such as Cisco Systems have turned acquisition into an art form, and some startups see product development as a conduit to a deal. Even without connecting quickly to the marketplace they hope that a Cisco will see and value their concept and buy it. Using its substantial marketing capabilities and influence, Cisco can then make that product a huge success. Having completed hundreds of such acquisitions over the past decade, Cisco grew into a behemoth by honing its strategy for integrating new companies and new technologies quickly and efficiently.

Cisco executive Charles Giancarlo, who oversaw many of the company's acquisitions during the 1990s, came to understand the nuances of product development. Harder than building a new product was convincing a customer that there was a return on investment in adopting that product. Most of Cisco's efforts were directed toward gaining customer acceptance of a particular product. Giancarlo came to see that building a company aiming to file a public offering is more difficult than building one to be sold.

"In order to go public, you have to build a value proposition that is compelling enough for a customer to implement the product," Giancarlo says. "And the product has to be substantial enough to be able to differentiate it from other products out there and support a sales and marketing organization to drive the product's success. That's very hard to do if what you have is a narrow niche product or one with a relatively low price."

In certain industry sectors, such as security or wireless devices, a raft of startups offer a variation on a theme, an enhancement to a mainstream product, for example. Such products may exist simply to offer that extra boost to an existing technology and thus those startups are prime for acquisition. A company like Cisco is constantly on the lookout for such opportunities because acquiring a strategic new technology is far faster and more efficient than developing it in house.

"We buy technology companies all the time," Giancarlo says. "Sometimes we look at a company and say, 'that's a technology, but not really a product.' Or we may say, 'that's a product, but not a company.' So there are various levels, and you can sell any of those. We buy companies with a product, but for one set of reasons or another, they were never able to create a company around that product to make it successful."

Having a strong business model and sticking with it, even during trying periods, can make product development decisions easier. Akamai Technology, which supplied servers to customers for deploying their Internet offerings, hit a wall when the Internet bubble burst. But by staying on its mission, it managed to survive and recover when the economy bounced back.

George Conrades, Akamai's CEO, points out that the young company survived its early-stage trauma because it was both a services and software company. "We're really a technology development company that manifests its value as a service," Conrades says. "In other words, we were selling software as a service long before it became popular."

With its core product fully developed and robust, Akamai was able to grow its business with incremental improvements delivered seamlessly. "The services model is one of sense and respond, which I love because we are constantly updating the network with new functionality and we're not waiting every six months for a new CD to go out," Conrades says. "As soon as product development has gone through quality assurance, we put it out online over the network."

Of course, early-stage startups can only look to survivors like Akamai with envy.

FAST, TOO FAST

In other cases, promising startups can be undermined by investor pressure to get a product to market before it is ready. John Landry, a Boston-based angel investor and technology executive, has worked with a dozen startups and has seen many variations of a theme. Most startups with a technology visionary driving the effort eventually face a critical challenge: when to build a team to start marketing and selling the product. In Landry's experience, timing is critical. Impatient venture investors may push hard for building out the team, but if they do, the startup may veer into trouble.

In one instance, Landry recalls, an entrepreneur with a strong product idea got early round financing from a venture capital firm. The VCs immediately pushed to bring in a high-powered management team, believing that a company is nothing more than the team. Pressured by the new team to rush the product into the marketplace, the startup shipped 250 beta offerings and got all 250 back. The product was not ready, customers angrily balked, and the management team eventually fled.

"You've got to finish what you start out to do," Landry states. "The product is critical. You can fail miserably if you bring it to market prematurely."

Today, entrepreneurs face even more daunting challenges in product development. The technical complexities of the technology environment and the pace of change in that environment create angst for product developers. It's tough to hit a moving target and to figure out which platform to develop the product for, the right language, the right operating system, the right channels and alliances. Startups must make large bets, and there is little time or resources for fighting internal battles.

Landry suggests hiring the best talent available but also to be careful about bringing in too many "really smart people." He is not being facetious. "With too many really smart people, you get the prima donna effect and you end up arguing how many angels you can fit on the head of a pin," Landry says. "And the work doesn't get done."

WHEN TO SPEND, HOW MUCH TO SPEND

A much trod-upon cliché in technology is underpromise, overdeliver. Building a product from its earliest demo stage to a fully realized, ready-to-ship version requires savvy insight that most technologists lack. We recommend that early-stage startups consider bringing in an experienced business development executive before hiring a marketing executive. (In the interests of keeping fixed costs down, we also recommend hiring a consultant to fill this role rather than a full-time employee.)

A good business developer is out in the field—the startup's area of interest—and is talking to prospective customers and is more likely to be in tune with emerging market opportunities than a pure marketing type.

In this mode, a startup has the opportunity to build value from the seed stage into later financing rounds as the product is being developed. The more tightly integrated the product development is with customer acquisition and input, the more value will be accrued for the nascent enterprise.

In this way, startups can better gauge how much to spend and when to spend it on research and development of the new product. Obviously, the startup must first address how much it can afford to invest and when. A company that is still cash flow negative has far shallower R&D pockets than a later-stage company that has achieved positive earnings. At cash flow negative, a startup is simply trying to minimize the burn rate and stay alive. At later stages, there will be plenty of feedback—from investors, customers, and analysts—telling an entrepreneur what level of R&D spending is required to remain competitive.

There is no fixed formula for R&D investment. Research-heavy industries like telecom and semiconductors have higher early-stage R&D requirements that must be factored in to any business plan. Dot-com survivors tend to reach product development maturity more quickly, as one might expect when the product is a hosted Internet service rather than a physical object that must be manufactured, packaged, and shipped.

Our research showed that, in general, going into a B round of financing, a startup has to have sold a product that can absorb at least $5 million to $20 million worth of rollup capital for the broader marketplace. This means that the value realization mechanism—the acquisition of customers, the meeting of product deadlines, the ability to avoid the usual "gotchas" that trip up many a business plan—has to be humming. As a startup makes its way through successive rounds of financing, this helps not only in attracting investment dollars but also helps defend a higher valuation. A higher valuation means giving up less equity in later financing rounds and thus avoids dilution for the founders.

So a company doesn't want to be entering a C round of financing with a partially developed product. By then, product development needs to be well along, with sufficient R&D funding to match sales to a core market and positive cash flow.

In recent years, since the bubble burst, there is little financing available for later rounds for startups without revenues. Today, companies are expected to have either real revenue or strong, defensible prospects of near-term revenue at the A round.

THE FINE POINTS

Product development, as we've stated, is not a finite experience but a multilayered evolution. Alignment around product development includes integral elements that are often ignored, but can trip up a development process and customer acquisition. Elements of functionality for the customer extend beyond the hardware, software, or service. There must a reliable service and support team and, of course, eventually a sales and marketing team to move the product into a revenue stream. Packaging, documentation, manufacturing, fixes for the inevitable bugs, and demonstration capabilities so that sales can properly show off the product all must be attended to correctly. Ignoring any of these factors can result in "gotchas" of the worst kind.

Startups should also consider adding a *customer satisfaction* objective to the list of key milestones in product development. Most companies consider the final ship date or volume shipment as the final milestone. But we believe this is a bad place to stop. A startup should only disband a product development team when it has validated that customers are getting what they want and need. There must be very concrete deliverables tied to that milestone. In fact, some of the best learning in the product development process occurs not when the team has frozen customer requirements but when a product begins shipping.

And since startups, even those seeking to be acquired, are not anxious to be labeled one-hit wonders, the product development vision must include product extensions, new products, and the ability to expand the customer base across multiple audiences.

"Once you get past the startup stage, you have the disadvantage of having a user base," John Landry says, only partially tongue in cheek. While existing products must be enhanced and moved across vertical markets, developers, if they are worth their salt, itch to be part of the next new thing. "Customers are incrementalists," Landry says. "They are never going to take you out to the next wave. You need a group doing that next wave, working on the future."

Successful startups find ways to keep the most talented developers involved in new research and offer avenues into these groups for developers working on extensions to current products.

In the long run, startups face the same challenge as more mature organizations. They want to be ahead of the market with product development, but not so far ahead that they run out of money before the market materializes. And they will succeed or fail based on the ability to execute. For startups and investors, great ideas poorly executed will undoubtedly fail. Good ideas executed well are enough to succeed.

As we shall see, product development, even executed well, goes hand in glove with customer acquisition, partnerships, and strategic alliances. These paths to value are inextricably intertwined.

## Ten

Customer Acquisition: You've Got to Have Someone to Sell Your Product To

In the mid-1990s, Sung Park, a software entrepreneur based outside Boston, began to build his first startup company. The embryonic venture was based on a software concept that would allow women, frustrated with the fit of off-the-rack jeans, to have blue jeans custom fitted using a desktop computer in a retail location. With the woman's measurements input into the system by a store clerk, the software created the dimensions for the perfect-fitting jeans and then automatically sent the coordinates to a factory in Tennessee where the jeans were cut, sewn, and shipped overnight to the customer. The startup, called Custom Clothing Technology Corporation, was on the cusp of a new wave of mass customization driven by telecommunications, software, and the Internet.

Park's initial venture investor, William Davidow, happened to live next door to the chief financial officer of Levi's, the clothing giant based in San Francisco. When Davidow walked over to his neighbor's house and explained the concept, there was immediate interest. Within days, Levi's vice president of marketing called Park and signed up as Custom Clothing's first customer. Levi's went so far as to fund part of the initial effort itself, and within eighteen months decided to acquire the company.

Though Levi's never built Park's idea into the success story he'd envisioned, it meant a lucrative exit strategy for Park and his investors. And though few startups can count on the residential serendipity of so strategically placed a venture capitalist, the story illustrates the importance of customer acquisition for a startup.

During the Internet bubble, one of the more amazing distortions of reality was how easily startup companies received funding based on a bare-bones business plan and without having signed a single customer. Venture money was flowing, and many of the basic tenets of value were discarded like yesterday's newspapers. But as the venture world returns to normalcy, startups are facing the kind of challenge that Custom Clothing faced. And they are once again aware of the importance of customer acquisition as a key metric of success. Finding and keeping customers as a startup works through its product development is crucial. A successful exit strategy, either through acquisition or an IPO, will depend heavily on a strong and entrenched customer base or, at the very least, a demonstrable *prospective* customer base.

WHAT WE FOUND

We found in our research:

- Among software and services startups, the more successful companies that had acquired initial beta customers and negotiated channel deals also had significant advantages along all the performance axes. Conversely, by the B round of financing, less successful companies had little channel activity, modest customer acquisition progress, and therefore little revenue. What we found most striking was the strong correlation among these companies between customer acquisition and cash flow.

- Successful software companies, not surprisingly, performed consistently better across the board on the customers, channels, and product development axes. Successful service companies did a much better job selling directly to customers than less successful companies. And the more successful software firms exploited direct sales, focused early on narrow markets, and were driven by markets rather than technology.

- The importance of early customer revenue, however, differed dramatically among industry groups. While early and consistently growing revenue was critical to service and software companies, telecommunications and semiconductor companies sometimes acquired beta and test customers that produced little revenue.

- For most startups, early "lighthouse" customers (who deeply believe in the company and will provide strong references) are crucial.

- Shorter sales cycles are better for startups. Generating more revenue over the course of a quarter allows a company to sell its product or service at a price that will achieve economies of scale and make further customer acquisition easier.

- And as we noted in earlier chapters, a more developed product does not necessarily lead to customer acquisition.

SEGMENTATION

Given that most technology startups are birthed by entrepreneurs with innovative ideas rather than marketers who see unmet customer needs, the push to acquire customers is often given less emphasis than it requires. The venture investors who make their bets on startups are usually the ones who bring reality to the table,

make key customer connections, and keep close tabs on the for-
mulation of customer acquisition plans. We noted in our research
that the most sought-after investor services were customer introductions and help in developing strategy and forming strategic
alliances.

————

ALEX OSADZINSKI

Partner, Trinity Ventures

Q: Do VC firms provide a service beyond simply providing
capital?

Osadzinski: We always ask ourselves, can we add value on
the board? Is there something we can actually help with or
do in an area where we have expertise? Do we know some
of the customers? Do we know people we can help hire?
The answer has to be yes, otherwise you're just showing
up and not adding value. Besides, someone who does add
value will get the deal done, and you won't.

Q: There is a lot of competition for deals?

Osadzinski: All of the good deals are competitive. The bad
deals are not. If someone is sitting in the lobby with an idea
for a perpetual motion machine, chances are he's sitting
there because he couldn't get funded anywhere else. But if
Jack Welch is sitting in the lobby with some engineers that
have some interesting ideas about how to improve manufacturing efficiency, I better damn well demonstrate I can
provide better service, better value, and bring something
to the board. I have to do that because I'll be competing
for that deal against fifteen other VCs.

Q: The rap on venture investors is that they think short term.
They want the fastest most profitable exit. Is that true?

Osadzinski: That's a myth. In fact, I believed it before I got
into venture. I thought if a venture investor could split a

company in two to double his investment, he would do it. But it's completely incorrect. Our investors—our limited partners—typically measure their investment on two dimensions: absolute return and internal rate of return.

Q: How does that change things?

Osadzinski: If you double your money in a year, that's 100 percent internal rate of return. But over the life of the fund, you only would have doubled your money once. That's because each dollar that comes into a fund only goes through it once. There's no recycling.

Say an investor commits $10 million to a venture fund. Over the life of a fund, they will send in checks for $10 million. We draw it down as we make investments. And over the life of the fund, the investor will get distributions. Each time a company is sold, shut down, or taken public, there's a distribution, an outcome. For each dollar that goes in, that dollar goes into some company, and whatever happens to that dollar, what's left of it, will come back to the limited partner.

And so, if over the life of the fund, that limited partner sends in $10 million and he only gets back $20 million, that's not that great. That's not why he invests in a venture. A venture investment typically is the highest risk, highest return type of investment. So if you ask most limited partners, if you send me $1 million, would you rather have back $2 million in a year, or $5 million dollars in five years, they'll tell you they want $5 million in five years. That's because their absolute return would be higher. That doesn't argue for short-term thinking.

Q: But you do hear quite a bit about how VCs are too short-term oriented.

Osadzinski: There are horror stories about VCs selling companies out from under management when management didn't want to sell. But you hear the opposite, too. Management wants to sell and the VCs don't want to for the reasons I've just outlined. What all this means is that entrepreneurs need to have boards that are not just made up of VCs. They need to have boards that have outsiders on them in addition to management and the VCs. The outsiders in particular tend to balance things out. On the other hand, you don't want a company where the board members are not aligned. You do need the board to be aligned. If the board is working effectively with the CEO and it's a collaborative relationship, good things happen. I've seen that more often than not.

Q: What metrics do you use between the seed and first round of financing to make certain things are on track?

Osadzinski: It's a mixture of gut and marketability. By that I mean the ability of the company to market itself. It's just like real estate. What are the comparable houses selling for? It's really, "What do you think this house is worth?" That is not to say there are no general rules and guidelines. There are. But the exceptions stand out. There are companies that defy gravity with valuations that really go up. Usually, it's because the CEO is very strong or the deal is very competitive.

Q: How long does it take?

Osadzinski: The typical investment process really takes three months. But of course some go faster. What makes them faster is that the CEO has just been there, done that, and is well known and has unimpeachable integrity combined with great results. That usually gets it going quicker and brings more money.

For those deals that are fundable in the seed round—and I define the seed round as a few hundred thousand dollars that you put in to see if there's anything there—many of them are done as convertible notes. There is no valuation. There are some disadvantages to it. VCs tend to like them because they're fair. You put in $300,000 and whatever the company is worth when they spend that $300,000 is what that $300,000 buys you of the company. Companies like it too because you don't have to haggle about it.

Think of it this way. Here you are in the A round. Let's say you raised $5 million and the company's worth $10 million now. But there's nothing there. There's a demo, a prototype, maybe some PowerPoint slides, five or six customers who say, "yeah, I think we'd try this." But it actually looks pretty good and we like the team. So we spend an hour on the phone with each potential customer, saying, "Who did you talk to, what do you think of them, what do you really think? How much would you really pay?"

So all of a sudden this thing is worth something based on a bunch of PowerPoint slides, some promises, and some enthusiasm. Great. Here comes the beast. Now you've got revenue. The revenue curve always says, $2 million, $10 million, $30 million, $100 million, or something like it. No one ever hits it.

And let's say that you're running $2 million a quarter in revenue. You spend that $5 million. Your first month, you only get $2 million—you just did a $2 million quarter. So you say, "Well, heck, you're at an $8 million run rate." The company's growing fast. It's worth at least $16 million, twice that. Maybe it's really growing fast. It's worth $20 million, $25 million in the current market. Everyone's happy. It was worth $10 million and now it's worth $20 million and it's making more money. Well, heck, that's a 2X step up in valuation. So everyone's happy. Dilution doesn't happen. Present account investors will ante up more and new investors will come in. All is peace and love.

But let's say that you spend the money and the market

didn't develop quite as fast as you thought and you just flung together a half million dollar quarter. This is much more normal. You say, "Oh dear. We made a good product, and the pipeline looks good." And you just hired a sales VP who's looking like he'll be good. But you're really at a $2 million run rate. That's pain.

In a sense, the company should really be worth more than it was before because it's made progress, it's hired people. Here too there's enthusiasm and promise. But now reality has set in. The company's actually now got product and customers. But it's only doing half a million dollars a quarter, a $2 million run rate. It may be worth $5 or $6 million, less than the $10 million it was at the last round.

So some bad things happen. They're going to get diluted. Previous investors don't ante up again. And pain results. The company may still continue, and many companies have devised ways to do that. But it's a pain.

Q: Revenue did not increase fast enough.

Osadzinski: Right. There was one quarter when, I think, almost none of our startups sold anything. It was Q1, '02. Customers just went away. It's so disheartening. It's bad enough for us as the investors, but I've been on the other side of the fence as an entrepreneur. You've put two or three years of your life into it, and you can see it all going away. It's very tragic.

It's better now. Companies are getting very savvy about not spending the money. You'll see a software company and you'll ask, "Where should $5 million take you?" I don't care what you're building, these days, $5 million should take you to $1 million a quarter in revenue. There's no reason why it shouldn't. Not unless you're building something huge.

What this means is that capital efficiency is coming back. Every entrepreneur knows this. Use this money, I don't care how you do it, but use this money to get to enough revenue and enough traction so you can do an up round—a round where you're valued higher—next time.

I'm just saying that early figures regarding valuation are based on promise, enthusiasm, the management team—what they did before and what they say they're going to do—and on how well they tell us they're going to do it. Valuations at later rounds tend to be based more on results.

Q: It sounds like venture investing has returned to its pre-bubble norm.

Osadzinski: A very large number of factors have returned back to normality. How equity is set between VCs and management. How management is compensated. Management can receive cash compensation, stock compensation. Valuation of the companies. The amount of capital required to get to certain milestones.

Capital is more efficient today. For the longest time, it took $15 to $20 million of capital to get an enterprise software company to profitability. During the bubble, it took between $50 and $75 million. Today it's back to the previous norm. So if a company comes in with a model that shows $10, $15 million to get to profitability, I'll believe it.

Q: How many companies do you fund each year? How do you find them?

Osadzinski: I will go to conferences, read about companies, talk on the phone, look at Web sites, and investigate 1,500 companies in a year, at least superficially. That's a lot of companies. In rough numbers, the firm itself will meet with probably 400 companies in a year, and we will invest in six or seven. Out of 1,500 companies, only six get funded. Some of the 1,500 will get funded by other firms—but not that many. Maybe 10 percent will get funded.

———

But the management team in a successful startup also has its eye on market size and sales cycles early in the game. As we've previously pointed out, startups require focus and a keen ability to identify market opportunities. One method for achieving this kind of focus is segmentation.

A lucid and articulate business plan will identify specific market segments and individual customers, and offer a blueprint for attacking the marketplace. Our research showed that startups often go after too many market segments simultaneously, trying to be all things to all people and fail to satisfy anyone. This is why a software powerhouse like Siebel Systems remains dominant in its market segment, customer relationship management software (CRM), more than a decade after its founding. It hasn't diluted its value proposition by going after markets in which it would be a second-tier player. In this regard, startups need to consider the GE theory set in motion by former CEO Jack Welch: Either be number one or two in a market segment or get out of that business.

In an era when information technology spending has plummeted and large corporate customers have cut back on investing in unproven new technology, simply getting a foot in the door has become a difficult task for a sales executive at a startup. Given the landscape, salespeople are forced to go after a broader segment of the population in the hopes of landing deals, even if those customers do little to grow or sustain the company.

Segmentation provides a mechanism for the type of strategic and competitive analysis that becomes a key driver to customer acquisition. Few startups have the discipline or focus to spend the required time on segmentation, but for those who do, the payoff is clear.

There are multiple ways to segment a market using simple and traditional measurements such as demographics, products, technology, and customer size. Is the concept driven better by big companies or small? Are these companies data-intensive or nondata-intensive? And there are also nontraditional ways to consider a market, which is always appealing to entrepreneurs. Park, for example, used psychographics to help determine what women like and how they buy things.

"For Levi's, we said we want to focus on females first by age, income, ability to purchase, and the percentage of those who had trouble finding blue jeans that fit the way they liked," Park said. The segmentation led to a target customer base of twenty million women and helped Park focus the company's message: "We were in the positive self-esteem business, not the software business."

The more a startup understands the needs of a certain segment, the more it can match its product attributes to those needs. Think of online services like Monster.com and Match.com or product offerings like TiVo. Jeff Taylor, founder of Monster.com, began the company with a business model that required Monster to act as a cobranded job posting link on the Web sites of bigger companies such as Ziff-Davis, Lycos, Excite, and *USA Today*. "We brought the career center and they would provide the traffic," Taylor says.

Eventually Taylor realized that Web users were more interested in going directly to destination sites, so he decided to change the business model and brand Monster.com as a stand-alone entity. And in order to reach customers, he decided to spend $3.2 million running ads during the Super Bowl. Prior to that decision, Monster had revenues of $40 million. Within three years it rocketed to $500 million.

And as we noted in the last chapter, this connection ends up driving the product development process as well. A startup that can match its product development to its customers' needs has a huge competitive advantage in any given market. If a product solves a big problem, this helps set the price strategy, which dovetails with the distribution strategy. All of this is driven by the segmentation process.

Martin Coyne, the lead director at Akamai, says that startups get in trouble by going after too many segments simultaneously. As our research showed, the successful startups tended to have a more narrow focus at the outset than the less successful companies.

"When you focus, amazing things can happen," Coyne says. As a senior executive at Kodak he led the company into the digital imaging era. Early on, Kodak tried to sell a raft of digital products and accessories, from cameras to CDs to ink jet printers. It found itself in several businesses, and the company's efforts floundered as a result. When Kodak's president confronted Coyne, he said he wanted Coyne to cut the business unit down to three products and jettison everything else. "I said, 'Are you crazy?' Coyne recalls. "He said, 'No, you need to focus.'"

Kodak sold off several of its businesses and decided to concentrate on digital cameras and ink jet photographic paper. The move has been a major win for Kodak and left a powerful imprint on Coyne. When he became a director at Akamai, he brought the wisdom with him.

With its Internet-based business model Akamai wanted literally to take on the world and set up international offices. Coyne was very vocal in his counsel. "Focus," he told Akamai's management team. "Every time you set up a business in another country, you've got to send somebody there. It's taking management time. It's taking the CEO's personal time. You've got to build relationships, worry about pricing, worry about transfer costs, transfer pricing, and what are you getting out of it?"

Instead, Coyne pushed the "Willie Sutton" laws of finance approach to customer acquisition. "Go where the money is," he suggested. "That's where you will find the customers," he said.

FINDING THE GUNSLINGERS AND THE CHAMPIONS

The question startups face early in their existence is what level of traction is enough to justify ramping up the investment in sales and marketing? The successful startups, especially in the post-bubble era, understand that their existence is essentially a race against insolvency. Every startup is in a battle against time and money, or the lack of both.

Facing a classic Catch-22 scenario, startups must try various approaches in order to find a product direction and strategic direction that works. But few have the luxury of the time and the money necessary for all those fits and starts that allow them to successfully jockey for position.

Veteran entrepreneurs who have been through the startup wars recommend finding a high-octane sales vice president early in the game. In the venture community, these types are called *gunslingers*, and they tend to have resumes that boast of a track record selling at least $5 million worth of one product after another. They've done this repeatedly throughout their careers.

"Every startup needs a gunslinger," Park says. "They're wild and impossible to manage, but to get past the gatekeepers, you need those kind of guys. You give them a phone and a Rand McNally atlas and let them go. They are key. If you don't get them, you never get those first few sales."

Startups with the best chance of success also need a champion inside that first key account. At Levi's, Park encountered David Schmidt, the vice president of marketing, who became a champion for Custom Clothing.

"He told us, 'I get it,'" Park says. "He funded us as a skunk works."

In a selling situation, a startup is likely to encounter four different constituents within a customer's organization: the person who makes the buying decision; the users of the product who always tend to influence the purchase; the technical screener who can press the "Keep Out" button; and the champion who, when the salesperson is gone, is internally selling your product to the company.

Given the ebbs and flows of the high-tech marketplace since the bubble collapsed, even the gunslingers are finding the markets more difficult to penetrate. Our research showed that the Internet bubble had a significant impact on customer acquisition. Companies that received financing in the bubble had made little customer progress by the A round. But companies that received financing *prior* to the bubble progressed more slowly, but had more customers by their A round. These companies increased in value as a result of customer success.

The postbubble recession had a profound impact on information technology spending, and CIOs not only slammed on the brakes on technology spending but put up vivid warning signs about spending on risky new products. The not-so-subtle message: *You make a mistake, you're fired.*

Naturally, for technology startups, the disappearance of corporate courage has created daunting barriers to entry. In a time when it became nearly impossible to find a champion—that one brave soul to carry an idea forward—startups have had to rethink their customer acquisition plans.

ARE CHANNELS BETTER?

Given that opportunities for one big score with a single client (e.g., Microsoft convincing IBM to embrace MS DOS for its personal computer) have become increasingly rare, startups have had to rethink customer acquisition strategies. We believe (as we will discuss in the next chapter) that channel partners and alliances have become the preferred entry into customer shops. For software and service startups intent on going it alone, a volume approach rather than seeking one cornerstone client is more likely to reap rewards. In software, for example, the perpetual license option is no longer preferred and may also be on the way to extinction.

Instead, packaging sales as subscriptions and as part of service offerings makes the product more palatable for IT executives who've been instructed to not add capital costs to the company's books. To this end, software leasing and online on-demand usage has begun to flourish.

Gregg Carman is a sales and marketing executive who has been involved in a raft of software ventures, and he suggests that the leading indicators of success in the current market are based on how many times a prospect is touched. *Touched* means face-to-face encounters, not simply phone conversations. One touch is okay, but more touches become meaningful by increasing the opportunities to land a customer.

Another leading indicator is how many prospects are in the sales pipeline who can actually be delivered? Given that, on average, it requires ten calls to land one visit, these touchpoints in the pipeline are the most significant indicator of customer acquisition.

Startups, Carman says, usually don't understand this aspect of sales. "The biggest problem I face are companies that say, 'Just get the revenue. Revenue heals all ills,'" Carman explains. "Instead, they should understand that revenue is really a lagging indicator. You have to hire people who know how to get to customers and know how to knock down doors. And you have to have a management team that believes in and is willing to invest in those things."

Listening to those customers and understanding their pain is another key for customer acquisition. Chief information officers (CIOs), when asked about best practices for getting in the door with a new product, tend to agree. Typically they say, "Don't offer me any capital expenses, because it's my job to have less vendors, not more. The minute you introduce a capital expense, even if it's $50,000, I have to get involved." During the darkness after the bubble, CIOs became terminally gun shy, unwilling to jeopardize their careers to promote unproven technologies.

Given that large corporate customers can pressure their own strategic vendors—the IBMs, Hewlett-Packards, Sun Microsystems—to come up with short-term solutions, even breakthrough or incrementally improved products are unlikely to win them over. Thus startups face the prospect of finding a backdoor entrance into the customer's world. Service-type solutions are one alternative. Finding an entry level where a purchase can be signed off by the lower level contact person rather than the CIO, or the CIO's boss, is also a plus.

Startups also must be careful what they ask for because they just might get it. Ron Bernal, a venture partner at Sutter Hill Ventures, worked for Cisco and says he learned a valuable lesson there. Cisco, he says, has always been a heavily customer-centric company, focused on customer needs. "Startups have to serve the customer," Bernal says. "You can't be focused on just the technology. You have to listen to your customer, figure out the critical pain points, and find a solution that has a high value."

Once a startup has cracked a key early customer, does it have the maintenance support structure in place to support its product? Can it support a cash flow structure that allows for longer, incremental deals over twenty-four months or more?

And will giant signature customers be more of a curse than a blessing? Carman recalls working with a startup in 1997 that was competing with several other vendors for a sale to Fidelity Investments, the mammoth financial services firm. Though his company won, Carman says that Fidelity is known "for sucking the life out of the profits of startups," and this particular startup only survived because it was acquired by Siebel Systems during its Fidelity contract. Carman says that Fidelity is hardly alone in its behavior with startups.

With the end of the bubble, a seller's market became a buyer's market, and startups were at even more of a disadvantage in convincing bellwether customers to take a chance. Selling your startup's soul in order to claim a marquee client may lead to the wrong kind of exit strategy.

Acquiring smaller customers in higher volumes in order to grow the company may well be a preferred road to success. Our research revealed that the more successful service firms focused early on *narrow* markets, exploited direct sales, and were driven by markets (customers and channels) rather than technology. The less successful firms had smaller progress with direct sales, tended to focus on broader markets, were driven by technology, and were founded at higher valuations.

CAPTIVATING A MARKET

One of the advantages of a startup is the ability to think outside the box and see markets where others don't. Experiencing an elevator ride as an advertising opportunity, for example, would not occur to many people. But for Mike DiFranza, that is the epiphany he had in the late 1990s when he founded Captivate Networks.

The Westford, Massachussets, startup, which we described in an earlier chapter, builds wireless, flat-screen video systems for elevators that provide both content and advertising for passengers in office towers around North America. From the early seeds of the idea, Captivate now has its screens in 4,500 elevators in twenty cities and makes its money selling advertising on the screens. As we noted in Chapter Six, Captivate estimates it reaches 1.4 million viewers each day. The company's business model has been so successful that it was acquired by the media giant Gannett in 2004.

Finding customers to buy his vision was not easy, but DiFranza believed in his basic premise and was able to build a convincing business case for the product. "It was obvious to us, even though it wasn't obvious to the rest of the world," DiFranza says. "We felt the ability for traditional advertising to reach consumers was becoming more challenged all the time. When we started the company in the middle of the Internet boom, we recognized that advertisers were looking for more efficient and effective ways to reach out to consumers. And we felt we could offer that through our media."

Beyond building the technology from scratch and convincing real estate companies to install the new systems in their office towers, Captivate had to acquire customers by convincing them that there was in fact a market opportunity in the small rooms that moved vertically throughout the day in the nation's office towers.

Though Captivate was going after advertisers rather than CIOs, its task was equally daunting. Traditional media buyers are not easily convinced to commit to and spend money on unproven new mediums. To build its case, Captivate had to prove the results ahead of time. Could the company convince media buyers that it had created a new and untapped medium that would attract a well-defined, high-end demographic that was not reachable in any traditional way?

The company's marketing efforts focused on the realities of traditional media, specifically that it was very effective on the bookends of the day—early morning, commute times, and late at night. But during the middle of the day, when businesspeople are at their most alert, traditional advertising has little impact.

Captivate invested significant expense to hire the Nielsen research firm to track the numbers, including not only how many people but how many elevator rides the average office tower employee took each day and how long those rides lasted. Nielsen conducted surveys as people stepped off the elevators to get real data on the impact of the advertising on the Captivate system. The results were impressive from an advertising perspective. Here was a vast audience whose total elevator time amounted to an average of six minutes a day, which translated into twenty-four hours a year. Because this target group has a high average income and education background, they were highly desirable consumers.

And like many startups, doing something new and unique means blazing a trail. Getting customers to buy something new and untried is always daunting, particularly in a bad economy. So DiFranza used his own high-tech sales background to target his audience. When contacting a prospective customer, who is the right contact point? The answer is the person with the pain, the person with a problem to solve. In this case, it was a vice president of marketing or sales. "He's the guy who's going to get shot if the company doesn't sell something," DiFranza says.

Captivate was able to make its advertising case to one big client and then began to land blue-chip customers such as IBM, Lexus, Staples, and McDonald's. In time, the customer list grew to be so impressive that Gannett made a buyout offer. Ironically, DiFranza thinks the bad economy helped Captivate's efforts. "If we had had a great economy when we were launching this business, we probably would be a much weaker company because we wouldn't have had to figure out what our real value proposition was," he says.

MATCHING THE VISION WITH EXPECTATIONS

Successful companies such as Captivate tend to make it for many reasons, but among the more subtle ones is the melding of an entrepreneur's *vision* with a customer's *expectations* of the opportunity. The founder's vision of the opportunity can end up informing and shaping the customer's expectations—think Federal Express and Amazon.com, for example. It's not simply a market sending a message to an entrepreneur—it's the entrepreneur educating potential customers and creating an opportunity in the market, much as Captivate or Dell or Craigslist.com have done.

In order to be successful, a founder has to adjust and create a path for the company to meet and embrace opportunities. Finding and winning over loyal customers in this way can mean the difference between success and failure. As a startup moves through financing rounds and accumulates these kinds of lighthouse or cornerstone customers, it becomes clear that these customers end up as opinion leaders who influence others or become the exit strategy in and of itself, as Levi's was for Custom Clothing.

In our follow-up study in 2003, we confirmed that customer acquisition was fundamental for the companies that received later rounds of funding. And for companies that moved up in status or development, it was also equally important—a logical step because the key measures of upgraded companies are shipping product and profitability.

As prebubble reason returned to the world of venture financing, startups seeking successful exit strategies understand that in order to even consider filing an IPO, a company must have real customers, real orders in the pipeline, and four or five quarters of consistently improving profitability. In other words, their valuation has to be based much more on actual results than upon a great marketing story.

As we will see in the next chapter, channel partners and strategic alliances are the safest and surest path to that plateau.

———

## Eleven

Never Walk Alone: Channels and Alliances

A lesson that cannot be overly stressed for startups is that early sales traction is table stakes to the game. The venture highway is littered with the rusting relics of wonderful technology that didn't sell.

No surprise, then, that our research showed that startups must forge early customer relationships on their own in order to have a reasonable chance at success. But in a technology environment in which new customers are difficult to land, particularly for startups, successful new ventures often turn to channels and alliances as the path to value.

Most technology startups, in order to survive until later rounds of financing, require a stamp of approval from the likes of Microsoft, Cisco, Hewlett-Packard, Dell, Oracle, SAP, Siebel, IBM, and a raft of other major technology players. Endorsements from the giants can carry a startup from obscurity to respectability far more quickly than can be accomplished with a solo effort. A giant channel partner can help alleviate the burdensome questions that customers aim at startups: Are you going to be around a year from now? Are you going to run out of cash? If I use your product or service, are you capable of supporting it?

According to our research, in the best-case scenario, a startup will find a mix of direct sales and channels and alliances in its quest for sustained growth and profitability. Our research revealed that the more successful software firms demonstrated a balance between channels and direct sales approaches. The less successful software firms had weak channel strategies. In a perfect world, startups should think customers first, channels second, alliances third.

But in times of economic uncertainty, when information technology spending is tight, management teams must create effective sales strategies in order to have any hope of a successful exit strategy. Veteran entrepreneurs always err on the side of caution, using conservative, prebubble metrics to approach a new market.

In our research we also found:

- Having acquired initial beta customers and negotiated channel deals, the more successful companies had significant advantages along all performance axes.

- Angel-backed companies gained substantial advantage along the channels/alliances and product development performance axes, while companies backed by venture capital focused more on customers.

- Less successful companies had little channel activity, modest customer acquisition progress, and little revenue.

- The most successful services companies did a much better job of selling directly to customers than less successful companies that attempted to bridge the gap by accelerating their channel strategy in the B round of financing. Successful service companies were driven more by markets (channels and customers) than technology.

KNOWING HOW TO SELL

One of the primary stumbling blocks for startups is an inability to understand just how a product will get sold. So many are focused on the technology development that they don't spend enough time thinking about who will buy the product, how they'll buy it, how much they'll be willing to pay, how they will pay, or how it will be distributed. Savvy venture investors spend a great deal of time focused on the sales model in the seed round or early financing rounds. Even the best product in the world will not sell if it is not distributed properly to its potential market.

Veteran investors like Alex Osadzinski of Trinity Ventures have seen a slew of successful and unsuccessful sales and marketing efforts among startups. Carefully sorting out the sales and marketing model within a given industry segment requires the kind of attention many startups fail to provide. Many believe they are solving the problem by adding a sales and marketing executive, but often a savvy business-development type is preferable.

"You have to really think about every element of the sales process," Osadzinski says. "A simplistic approach such as 'We'll sell it direct and then go through channels later' is pretty daring. Some products can only sell direct, some through channels. Not figuring that out at the beginning can be very dangerous."

The paths to value in the channels and alliances metric vary greatly depending on the product and the industry. A software startup, for example, has a far different set of needs and parameters than a biotech startup. Startups selling services or new hardware face different hurdles than software vendors.

All startups, however, must consider several crucial issues:

- How do you demonstrate the value and risk of your venture to potential investors? From an investor's perspective, there is a significant increase in value and reduction in risk if channels and customer relationships are being built effectively early on. If there is a strong commitment behind the channel or reseller relationship and the product or service is strategically aligned, a startup's value is enhanced immeasurably. A channel partner with a strong interest in bringing a product or service to the end customer, who sees that product or service as critical to their own strategy, will be a cornerstone relationship for the startup.

- In order to convince channel partners of the value of a relationship, the startup must demonstrate performance capacity and the unique value the product offers that makes a difference in the market. Three PowerPoint slides will no longer suffice—as it might have during the bubble—to convince prospective channel partners. A startup must not only be able to demonstrate the technology but also provide evidence that it can win over customers to prove that the technology is worth an investment. Documented customer interest, including testimonials, is vital to luring channel partners.

Startups should consider bringing on board people who have worked for a prospective channel partner or at the very least the industry in which the channel partner operates. Channel partners often evaluate more than just a product: they also want to know who is working for the startup. A former employee who deeply understands that market segment is a way to achieve early credibility.

ALLIANCES AND BEYOND

Adesso Systems, a mobile computing application development software startup in Boston, is aiming squarely at Microsoft's next Windows release. John Landry, the company's cofounder and chief technology officer, points out that alliances with power-houses like Microsoft are crucial to a startup's viability.

"We're in the early release program, and we've used their developer's kit to infiltrate our way into Microsoft's new environment," Landry says. "They want to have companies with them to showcase how we've used the new Microsoft technologies to build our new products. We want to be in there because it's not just an endorsement, it's the public relations value and the chance to be part of their marketing."

Adesso has established similar alliances with Hewlett-Packard and several other technology partners.

Alliances such as these, while valuable for startups, may be less enticing for venture investors. Startups routinely sign up for a nominal fee to be part of a development program for major vendors. But such alliances are not enough. Figuring out exactly what an alliance means is crucial for a management team. Simply enrolling in development programs doesn't guarantee the type of interconnection with a vendor that will impress an investor.

While the line between channel partners and alliances tends to blur, the test is *whether the development agreement will have a real impact on a new product.* An alliance can mean anything from a simple press release to a serious joint development, joint sales, and sell-through opportunity. Channels are explicitly about getting a product sold. Alliances may be more indirect and thus less effective.

Investors warn that an alliance is not a straight channel sale. Rather, it brings something else to the table, something softer, more about marketing lead generation than direct sell-through of a startup's product. Some alliances result in incorporating the startup's product into a vendor's product, which is a form of a channel, but one that is much more difficult to make money from.

Alliances with systems integrators, for example, have great potential for certain startups. A product that must be integrated or adapted and customized into larger systems in order to work in a customer's location will likely end up in the hands of a systems integrator eventually. Creating alliances with large systems integrators such as EDS, Deloitte & Touche, or KPMG can be a foundation for success. Software startups will bring in people from the systems integrators as early employees, and these people can end up as invaluable conduits to the systems integrators, educating them about products, creating sales opportunities for them as part of large integration projects.

Osadzinski worked with Vitria Technology, a software startup that hired several people from the systems integrators, and as a result the company made several successful alliances with systems integrators. "This catapulted sales through the roof," he says. "More than half our sales came from alliance partners."

In order to create a valuable alliance, startups should:

- Figure out up front what you want out of an alliance. Be very clear about what the goal is. Determine what you and the alliance partner will get out of the deal. There is no such thing as a "smart" *one-way* alliance partner, according to Osadzinski. "There are dumb one-way alliance partners who get nothing out of it, but those are not the partners you want," he says.

- Focus on alliances with quantifiable results. Joining a development program may bring good publicity, but a press release announcing a joint effort does not necessarily spawn customers or revenues.

- Target alliances that will move your sales curve up and to the right.

For example, one of Trinity Ventures' startup companies signed a significant alliance with Cisco Systems. The startup makes a product that helps test, certify, and monitor voice-over IP installations, a new technology sector in which Cisco is a leading vendor.

Cisco acts as a primary source of lead generation for the startup because the networking giant knows where the voice-over IP systems are being installed. Cisco's sales force recommends the nascent company to its customers as well, which makes the alliance extremely significant for the long-term success of the startup. For Cisco, the startup solves a difficult problem in allowing customers to certify and test their installations. It's a win-win situation for both companies, and given Cisco's penchant for acquisition it might lead to a desirable exit strategy.

In this regard, it is important for startups to *treat their alliance partners as customers*. The startup must be able to identify the partners' needs and pain points. Based on this relationship, the startup must design the needs of the alliance partner around not just the relationship but also the product or service elements themselves.

The management team must ask itself: If my alliance partner is a selling channel for us, how can we make it easier for them to sell our products or services? Can the product be easily demonstrated? Is there training available? Collateral material available? Is there a meaningful pricing strategy? Is the product robust and ready to be shipped? The same kind of care needed to tend to customers is needed here. Venture investors and consultants express amazement how often this aspect of such important relationships gets left unattended.

AVOID CHANNEL OBSCURITY

As much as they may come to depend on channel and alliance partners, startups must make sure that they never let channel partners shield them from their customers. Veteran entrepreneurs understand the danger of allowing a channel partner to obscure the direct feedback from customers by filtering that information before it reaches the people who are responsible for a product or service.

Startups must continually build knowledge databases about their customers and hear firsthand how a customer is using a product, what problems or issues are arising, and what future development direction a product must take. In this, having interests aligned with a channel partner is critical. For example, a startup may be a product company that wants to make its offering as easy and profitable as possible for its customers to use. A channel partner may believe its margins are in the extra work; the more difficulty a customer has in deploying a product, the more billable hours it might be able to charge. A practical feedback loop established at the outset of a partnership is a key requirement.

Although a startup may find it difficult to resist the lure of a single giant channel partner and the attendant credibility that might bring, the management team must understand the risk of being a tiny fish in a huge pond. Industry leaders like Cisco, HP, or IBM, which sell thousands of products and services to millions of customers, are unlikely to focus much time and attention on a small startup's offering, which represents just a minuscule fraction of their business. Can startups hope to gain enough mindshare in this relationship to make it worthwhile?

Do they trade off the closeness to their customers for the ability that a giant channel partner offers to scale up more quickly and effectively? Given that such a partner will undoubtedly seek exclusivity in any deal, is this a pact with the devil or a smart long-term business strategy?

Investors seeking a path to value will ask a series of questions about these very relationships: How clearly developed is the business strategy? Has the startup mapped out the value chain, evaluated the importance of channel partners, and where will the cash flow come from through these partners? Is there money in these deals? Is there a feedback loop from customers to the startup integrated into the deal?

MAKING CHANNEL CHOICES

Investors pay close attention to a startup's strategic position in any given marketplace. A startup's valuation is affected by whether or not it is dependent on channel partners, and if so, what potential exists in the marketplace. One startup in the Trinity Ventures portfolio makes CMOS radios and power amplifiers for cell phones. Osadzinski points out that his firm was well aware, prior to investing, that there are just five or six key cell phone manufacturers, such as Nokia, Motorola, and Samsung, that count as far as the startup's future is concerned.

These cell phone makers are not only customers but also partners because they will tout the benefits of cell phones using the startup's technology to the telecommunications carriers. "It doesn't matter how many second-tier cell phone makers you sell to," Osadzinski says. "If you don't have good relationships with these five or six manufacturers, you are dead in the water. Your valuation is nothing."

Sometimes it is the partnerships that startups avoid that can make the long-term difference. When Captivate Networks began to install its systems in office tower elevators, the first prototype went into an Otis elevator. Otis, the world's dominant elevator manufacturer, was so impressed with the technology that it asked Captivate for an exclusive deal. Michael DiFranza, Captivate's founder and CEO, refused. It was a gut check decision. "Here we were. We have no revenue, very little funding, a cool technology, and an idea," DiFranza says. "And here is the largest elevator company in the world that wants to partner with us, and we said, 'No.'"

DiFranza displayed the kind of wisdom not often found in startups. The fact that Captivate viewed itself as a media company rather than a technology company drove the decision. In any given market, DiFranza discovered, Otis has about a 25 percent market share. "That meant that if I partnered only with Otis, the most penetration I could get in any given market was 25 percent, even if I had 100 percent of their elevators. I wanted 100 percent of the market. I want to reach everybody in that downtown corridor. That was one of the most important decisions we *didn't* make."

Ironically, but not surprisingly, Otis chose to jump in and compete head to head with Captivate, despite the patents Captivate held on the technology. Otis's effort was a failure, reaching a peak of one hundred elevators, while Captivate expanded to 4,500 elevators. When Otis quit the business, Captivate replaced all the Otis systems and went on to become an Otis partner. In fact, just as Otis was deciding to sign up as a partner under Captivate's terms, the startup was beginning a round of financing. The Otis deal drove up the valuation significantly.

Unfortunately, most startups don't have the vision or the clout that Captivate displayed. Playing chicken with giant competitors is not for the faint of heart. In most cases, startups turn to the business development executive on its management team to guide it through these treacherous waters.

A top-notch veteran business development specialist is a key member of a team. But this can be a tough position to fill. A great business development person will figure out the "mental map" of how a product or service will get to the eventual paying customers and figure out what alliances will generate sales. A marginal business development type will do a lot of lunches and issue a lot of alliance press releases without the necessary results.

In the world of startups, business development is not always recognized for the critical role it plays. It is not uncommon for founding teams to marginalize a team member by handing him the title of vice president of business development. Osadzinski says this often becomes code for "Vice President of No Smoking in the Lobby" or "Founder That We've Shuffled Off and Hope He'll Eventually Go Away."

"I don't see very strong business development capabilities in startups," says Martin Coyne, lead director at Akamai. "I see people who can do deals and contracts. But I don't see strong people who can go out and really sing through business development strategy. It impacts partners, channels, and in some cases customers."

Coyne suggests that business development is a skill that can be integrated into a startup as a variable rather than a fixed cost. Changing business models, downsizing, and a difficult economy have put many strong business development professionals out on the street, and thus many would gladly take project work with small companies or startups.

CONCLUSION

In the Darwinian world of startups, where survival of the fittest means those who've built up enough sales traction to make it to another round of financing, channels and alliances can be life preservers. In order to connect and thrive with partners, startups should focus on the following:

- Think about the customer—how they buy, what they buy, why they buy, who they buy from, how much they will pay, and how to get them into the fold. Within this framework, think how a channel or alliance partner will help.

- Consider the economics of your sales model. Be realistic. A startup that believes it can sell a $300,000 enterprise software package through direct sales is living in a dream world. Big customers don't buy those kinds of packages from startups.

- Focus on the win-win for both channels and alliances. There is no worthwhile alliance that is a one-way benefit for either party. There has to be benefit for both or the partnership won't work.

As our research revealed, the most fit survivors are those who combine strong direct customers sales with potent channel and alliance partners. As with all the metrics in this study, execution is easier said than done. Hopefully this blueprint for maneuvering through the morass of startup angst and calamity will provide some needed guidance and support.

## Twelve

What We Know Now: Why Startups Succeed

Over the past several years that we have been studying startups we learned a lot that is interesting and even more that's useful. We learned that all startups are different, and that while there are no hard and fast rules that you can follow in order to succeed when starting a company, there are at least some rules of thumb that you can employ for advantage. We also learned that there are degrees of success.

Most successful entrepreneurs we talked to either grasped these rules of thumb intuitively or they learned them from experience. In some cases, newly minted entrepreneurs were taught the ropes by their investors, friends, and even by those they employed.

Let us distill from our research, case studies, and interviews the ten rules of thumb we've learned:

1. *Start with a large group of three or four founders,* the way Unica's founder Yuchun Lee did. The larger the group, the better its chances. If possible, it's best if the founders previously worked together at the same company. This is important because a larger group comes with a larger skill set and with access to capital. Since hiring the right team

takes a long time, starting with a team that's worked together before increases the speed at which the company can grow. In the startup world, the best leaders are those that know how to share power rather than those that have a need to take it all. The best people to lead startups are those that think building something is more important than winning prestige.

2. *Make certain a marketing or sales person is a member of the founding team,* as MIT's Edward Roberts found out in his research. Companies make big mistakes when they focus all their resources on their products and services but not their markets. If the company being started is technical, don't worry if the technologist and marketers disagree. You need them both even though they see the world differently. In startups, when conflicts arise, they have to be argued out or mediated toward a creative conclusion, not simply stopped.

3. *It's all about teams,* as Millennium's Mark Levin suggests. Whether you are starting with a group that's worked together in the past or hiring a team from scratch, successful entrepreneurs get that way because they can create teams. To some this may be intuitive; to others it requires reasoning and lots of hard work. Either way, hiring the right team is critical. In high-performance teams, managing each team member's rivalries is also critical. To get the right people on board requires painstaking due diligence and reference checking. The best time to start interviewing people is long before you start a company. Build a network of talented people around you upon which you can draw when you start to build a company. Do it at work, through networking, and with your investors. Super success comes from building super teams.

4. *When building the business, don't worry about your exit,* as Sutter Hill Ventures' Ron Bernal says. Concentrate on creating value. Entrepreneurs that focus too much on exit strategies lose their focus. So do entrepreneurs that worry too much about diluting their ownership stake. Creating high levels of value has a way of making even wrong things right. The best venture capital investors look for bigger, longer-term payoffs, not just quick results.

5. *Manage your cash,* as Alex Osadzinski of Trinity Ventures argues. Startups in the bubble years burned through money, but companies today have to be run much more tightly. Startups are a highly speculative investment, and at each stage of an investment's life, the people leading the company must know how much money it will take to increase revenue and become profitable. Young companies need high levels of financial discipline even more than older, established companies. Why? Because their margin of safety is far more tenuous and postbubble investors remain wary.

6. *Start with a market,* as Mike DiFranza of Captivate did. Occasionally a product or service will be so innovative or revolutionary it will create a market on its own. But for the most part, startups become successful not by creating markets but by going into markets that already exist, with a twist. They develop products or services that are better, easier, or cheaper. They also succeed by automating processes that were once done by hand. The common factor, however, is that no startup succeeds by being too inwardly focused. New companies must really understand the markets they are entering. That is the only way they can create tangible results.

7. *Find a great first customer,* which is what Jamie Rapperport of Vendavo did. A great first customer gives a startup big bragging rights. It also creates confidence in the market. Even so, you won't get a great first customer unless you can win their trust. Great customers only want to work with companies they are certain will stay in business. Success loves nothing more than success.

8. *Build a board that is a great "sounding board," not just a good watchdog,* as George Conrades at Akamai did. Boards are there to help companies create value by making introductions, assessing plans, and opening up their Rolodexes to management. The best boards are those that really focus on helping management solve its thorniest problems—and then get out of the way. Venture capital investors are a mixed bag when it comes to sitting on boards. Some have lots of experience and deep insights, while others are stretched too thin. Choose your board members wisely and make them work as partners in building your company's success. As you build your board, shape it into a group of problem solvers with smarts, deep pockets, and lots of business acumen.

9. *Make your product or service high quality and unique, then brand it in a way people won't forget,* as Monster's Jeff Taylor did. At first, people hated the Monster name; even so, they didn't forget it. Soon, it became synonymous with searching for a job.

10. *Enjoy the ride.* Without exception, the entrepreneurs we interviewed—and the people who funded them—loved what they did. They had passion, vision, and an ability to shrug off their mistakes and move on. They exuded confidence. They took pride in building things and in seeing their teams and their companies prosper. And

while many were highly technical, they were also people who, for the most part, really enjoyed being with other people.

Simply following these ten rules of thumb will not guarantee success. You need good ideas and you need good timing. You need money and you need the ability to generate enthusiasm. You need energy—and the capacity to work long hours and stay up late. You need to believe in what you are doing and you need to believe in yourself. You also need to remember that speed trumps perfection.

Still, after years of research, we can say that if you follow these ten rules of thumb and the rules at the end of each chapter, your chances of success are certain to increase.

Epilogue

The research upon which this book was based represents one of the largest and most comprehensive studies of startups ever conducted.

We began our research effort just as the Internet bubble was beginning to burst—and we did this for a reason. We felt that we would find out more of what was useful from companies that were trying to navigate through challenging times than we would by studying companies that succeeded when times were favorable.

Though the myth is that most startups fail, the reality is brighter. A high percentage of startups survive, which is to say that they do not go out of business within the first year or two. Another group does well, and a small percentage of startups thrive. Surprisingly, even during those very turbulent times, the overall success rate for the startups we studied was relatively high, as we indicate below. Depending on how success is measured, an entrepreneur who begins a business with open eyes and a modicum of skill has a better chance of succeeding than of going broke. More than half of all businesses we studied survived for more than five years. Many of them survive to this day.

In 2002, one year after the initial interviews, we reinterviewed executives to determine how their companies had progressed. We examined whether additional rounds of funding were achieved. (Achieving a new round of funding is an indication that valuation had gone up and that a company's prospects for the future were viewed as positive by investors.) We also determined whether changes—positive or negative—in business status or business development had occurred. For example, a company could occupy one of four stages of business: 1) in product development, 2) product in beta test, 3) shipping product, or 4) profitability. With regard to business status, a company could be private and independent, merged or acquired, public, in bankruptcy, or out of business.

To reflect these additional findings, we created a new set of Star Charts to compare the characteristics of the companies that successfully completed another round of funding with those of companies that did not. We also compared the Star Charts of companies based on changes in business status or development. The Star Charts throughout this epilogue are placed side by side to facilitate comparison.

As we conducted our 2002 research, we conclude—as this book has shown—that the business model is a key factor that leads to success in early-stage companies. We also concluded in 2002 that the business model and product development are very important determinants for obtaining additional funding rounds. The two go hand in hand. To raise money, it's not enough to structure a business correctly; you also need to develop products within the correct time frame.

In addition (also in 2002), we further verified that understanding the market for a good or service is critical to a startup's success. Overestimating market size and developing products poorly stood out as key factors in the failure of early-stage companies to obtain additional venture capital funding.

In June 2003, we released a short paper (its findings are listed below) that showed the rates of success in the universe of companies we studied. Throughout this exercise, we also invited investors to list all of their investments in a secure, password-protected online site. This secure site gave us confidential data on more than one hundred companies.

In 2004, we developed case studies and a smaller sample of in-depth interviews with CEOs of startups that had survived at least four years. We also interviewed investors. The goal of our research in 2004 was to distill from the companies we studied lessons that could be put to use to increase a startup's chances of success.

At the end of 2001, 23 of the 351 companies in the study group were already bankrupt or had gone out of business, which left us with 328 companies. Of these 328 companies in business at the time of our June 2003 research paper, 135 companies had success-fully obtained a new funding round following the study. Fifty-three of the 328 experienced an upgrade, and 18 underwent a downgrade. (Sixteen went bankrupt and two had experienced a negative change in business development.)

Considering the period in which we were conducting this re-search, we were pleasantly surprised that only 18 companies out of 328 had either gone bankrupt or had a serious negative busi-ness development. Because such a large share of companies had survived in such difficult times, we made plans to begin case studies and interviews to delve deeper into what entrepreneurs and investors can do to increase their odds of success. The table below, first presented in June 2003, summarizes by industry sec-tor the percentage of companies that were successful in their ef-forts to raise new money and increase their valuations.

Industry	Success Rate
Telecom	59%
Semiconductors	57%
Software	39%
Services	31%
Biotech	30%
Average	**38%**

As we examined these findings, we arrived at a number of con-clusions based on success-rate differentials by sector. Telecom and semiconductors are research-intensive industries with concrete products intended for development. These characteristics indicate a greater resilience to the downturn of the dot-com industry than that exhibited by software companies and even more so by services companies. The higher ranking with regard to additional funding for telecom and semiconductors is not surprising. However, the bottom ranking for biotech companies is curious. It is possible that the biotech companies, which often spend a decade developing a product, had sufficient resources from their early rounds that reduced or eliminated their need to seek additional funding. Their higher scores in cash flow during later rounds would suggest this. Of all the industry groups, services companies had the lowest scores in cash flow.

Chart 2. Upgraded Versus Downgraded Company Results

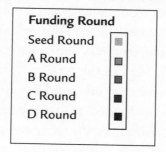

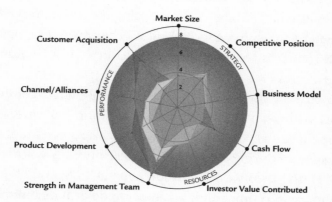

Upgrades = 54 companies

Source: PricewaterhouseCoopers

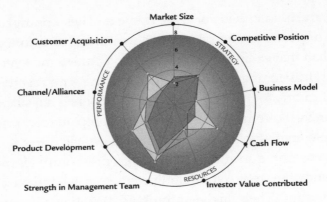

Downgrades = 18 companies

Source: PricewaterhouseCoopers

A very notable distinction among the downgraded companies is that they did not make it to the later rounds. Accordingly, we can only compare the upgraded companies and the downgraded companies for rounds seed through B.

The companies that achieved upgrades (those moving up in status or development) showed advantages in competitive position and stronger scores for business model and market size for the three rounds for which they could be compared. Upgraded companies also had stronger scores during the seed and A rounds for customer acquisition and cash flow. They scored higher during the B round in channel alliances and in investor value contributed.

Under these terms of comparison, the upgraded companies stood out with regard to customer acquisition and strength of management teams. Upgraded companies also scored higher for channel alliance during the C round. These findings were echoed in our 2004 discussions with entrepreneurs, CEOs, and investors. Among upgraded companies, business model stands out relative to downgraded companies. Market size also stands out significantly for the upgraded companies. The inference is that the upgraded companies made market size estimates appropriate for their respective business models. The result is a powerful combination leading to a successful upgrade for the company.

Competitive position for the A and B rounds and cash flow in the seed and A rounds also surface as extremely significant. Investor value contributed is greater in the B round for the upgraded companies, compared to the downgraded companies, but this does not indicate a significant pattern.

To summarize, these comparisons suggest that once an early-stage company creates momentum with its product because of a sound business model and an accurate estimation of the market, customers and the management team overshadow all other axes when it comes to creating value.

Over the past five years, we have observed hundreds of startup companies in various stages of growth. During that time we interacted with hundreds of entrepreneurs and dozens of investors. We met in good times and we met in turbulent times. And when we did, we talked about success and the ever-present threat of failure. We also talked about dreams.

The research process that we undertook was exhaustive, but if truth be told, it was also inspirational. The economies of great nations are ultimately built on the sweat and toil of a few people who believe in themselves so much that they are willing to risk everything to start a company. They work through the night, they start in garages, they mortgage their homes, they fail, and then they start again.

But not only are they inspirational: entrepreneurs—and the companies they start—are engines of progress that affect us all.

Over the last five years, we watched 350 companies start from scratch and grow. In the next five years, hundreds—even thousands—more will likely be started. Some of those new businesses will fail. But among those that succeed, one or two may actually change the world.

—

Appendices

Appendix 1. Paths to Value Study

A. Summary of Findings
B. Paths to Value—Introduction
C. Industry Descriptions and Comparisons
D. Market Environment
E. Regional Aspects of Early-Stage Financing
F. Role of Investor
G. Conclusion

How Does Your Company Compare?

Appendix 2: A Brief Primer on Venture Financing
Appendix 3: Survey Sample and Methodology
Appendix 4: Definitions of Performance Categories
and Axes of Value

A. SUMMARY OF FINDINGS

Since the boom of the late '90s, the venture capital industry has changed substantially for both venture capitalists and entrepreneurs. Many startups that shone brightly during the glory days of the Internet tech-stock bubble either have failed to survive or have seen their value evaporate at an alarming rate as the venture "bust" supplanted the venture boom. The year 2001 saw a dramatic decrease in investment in new companies as venture investors focused on their existing portfolios and questioned their approach to early-stage financing. Now, in the year 2002, the industry needs to take stock. It needs to question seriously how, in light of new economic and political realities, value is created among early-stage companies and, more important still, how it is sustained.

While such an exercise is clearly needed, early-stage companies and their investors face a unique challenge. Many metrics and diagnostic models exist for the evaluation of public companies, but few have been put forward to test the success of new ventures in various industries operating under various strategies. And those few, where they exist, are closely guarded and sheltered from public discussion and dialogue.

The Paths to Value model emerged in response to this challenge and to the inevitable questions that arose: Do traditional approaches to early-stage value creation still apply? Can consensus be reached on the kinds of metrics relevant in an essentially new economic landscape? Given the upheavals in the venture capital industry in the last three years, the need to confront these questions and to provide answers has become urgent. And the time to do so is now.

The Paths to Value model in this book was constructed by the authors on the basis of research and experience in the early-stage venture market. It captures the state of a company at a point in time through measurements of distinct components of company performance, capability, and business focus, and through the integration of these measurements into a single chart.

To validate and apply the model, we conducted an extensive survey and analysis of more than 350 companies that received seed and first-round private financings in the years 1999, 2000, and 2001—a period of huge market changes. The model attempts to identify specific strategies for sustained value creation among early-stage companies operating in a variety of industries and regions and under differing market conditions. Because we relied on interviews with entrepreneurs and executives of early-stage companies rather than on information obtained from venture capital partnerships, we believe that our findings are more representative than many other analyses.

Broadly speaking, venture creation involves two activities: choosing an opportunity and acting on it. We decided not to focus on the choice of opportunity because the many factors in play tend to defeat generalization, and no model can reliably predict the next great value opportunity. We also did not attempt exact return on investment calculations; longer-term studies are needed to capture credible information in that regard. However, by eliminating these concerns we were better able to recognize a most fruitful area for study. We set the goal of constructing a realistic framework for understanding value creation and determining the steps taken by investors and management teams to increase value between rounds of financing (measured as a multiple of initial valuation). We believed that we could also reach for a much better understanding of industry, regional, and market-timing phenomena.

Some of our conclusions in194 the resulting study simply underscore or deepen the common wisdom concerning new ventures. However, there are also new and distinctive insights. As well, we believe that the Paths to Value model and diagnostic approach provide significant promise for additional insight over the long term and offer a starting point for public discussion concerning the valuation process as it applies to early-stage companies.

The Paths to Value Approach

Paths to Value is a new approach to measuring the developmental progress of early-stage companies, based on two diagnostic tools: a set of metrics that we refer to as axes of value, and the Paths to Value Star Chart, which provides clear visualizations of these metrics for both individual companies and groups of companies.

Axes of Value

The nine axes of value used in this survey are distributed equally among three key factors: *strategy, resources,* and *performance.* With respect to strategy, they are market size, competitive position, and business model. In the area of resources, they are cash flow, investor assistance, and management team. For performance, they are product development, customer acquisition, and alliances/distribution channels.

The Paths to Value Star Diagram

Survey data related to the axes of value are plotted on a Star Chart:

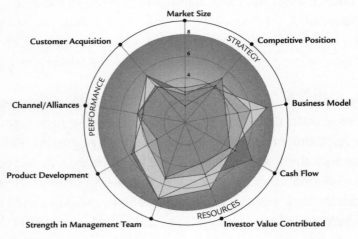

Source: PricewaterhouseCoopers

This approach to modeling has proved to make immediate, intuitive sense to participants in and observers of early-stage, venture capital-backed startups. It enables analysis and comparison among groups of companies selected according to different criteria, such as industry or degree of success.

When we compared companies that were successful with those that were less so, patterns of success emerged. These patterns can help answer the questions with which early-stage investors and management teams most need help, questions such as:

- When should I invest more in further developing my product?

- How and when should I engage channels?

- What level of customer traction justifies investment in ramping up sales?

- What should be the balance between growth and profitability?

- How developed were other companies in my industry when they successfully raised a particular round of financing?

Key Findings: Overall

In this initial effort to trace the Paths to Value among early-stage companies in the venture capital industry, we looked at various firms operating in different industries and regions under changing market conditions. For purposes of comparison, we sometimes grouped research and development-intensive companies (semiconductor, telecom, and biotech) and service-intensive companies (software and services). We also looked at a number of dot-coms that classified themselves as software or services companies, and analyzed them as a separate category. The regions considered were the United States and Europe (including Israel). We also looked at the impact of market conditions before, during, and after the Internet "bubble," and contrasted firms by degrees of success measured as changes in value over time. The following are among the key findings that emerged:

- Clear contrasts exist between the patterns of the most and least successful companies in our sample.

- On average, the more value a company created, the more accelerated was its progress along the Paths to Value.

- The Paths to Value of the most successful companies were industry-specific.

- The success patterns of R&D-intensive companies (biotech, telecom, and semiconductor) differed dramatically from those of service-intensive companies (software and services).

- The Paths to Value model offers a genuinely revealing diagnostic tool in identifying key developmental milestones that successful companies should strive to achieve at various rounds of financing.

Key Findings: By Industry

A number of important differences—some of them counter-intuitive—emerged by industry:

- General

  - The importance of early-customer revenue differed siginificantly among the industry groups studied. Early and consistently growing revenue was critical to services and software companies. On the other hand, biotech companies had little revenue during an extended R&D period. Furthermore, telecom and semiconductor companies sometimes acquired beta and test customers that produced little revenue.

  - Industry characteristics determined the degree of emphasis placed by an early-stage company on its technology, channels, and customers.

- Telecom and Semiconductor

  - The most successful firms raised their seed financing with larger identified markets and benefited from high levels of steadily increasing value.

  - Less successful firms raised their seed financing at higher valuations and emphasized well-developed products and strong early competitive positions. At initial financing, these companies were actually farther along than successful companies on the product development axis and perceived themselves to be in stronger initial competitive positions. By later financing rounds, however, the more successful companies had moved ahead of their less successful counterparts on most measurements.

  - Firms that were more successful availed themselves of higher levels of investor assistance, and these levels increased steadily at each round of financing.

- Software

  - The more successful firms as a whole demonstrated a balance between channels and direct sales approaches.

  - The less successful firms had weak channel strategies.

  - The most successful companies paid more attention than their less successful counterparts to growing revenue and to building scalable business models. These companies also made greater and steadier progress on the product development value axis.

  - A more developed product is not always better. A large number of the failed software companies achieved significant product development as they burned through investor dollars without achieving robust progress in customer acquisition and cash flow.

- Services

  - The more successful firms exploited direct sales, focused early on narrow markets, were driven by markets (customers and channels) rather than technology, and experienced low seed and A round valuations.

  - The less successful firms did not have as much success with direct sales, tended to focus on broader markets, were driven by technology, and were founded at higher valuations.

- Dot-Coms, Services, and Software Combined

  - Successful firms showed strong cash flow and scored high on all value axes.

  - At the seed stage, the most successful companies scored higher on all value axes but two: market size and strength of management team. The less successful companies excelled along these value axes. Once startups acquired initial beta customers and negotiated channel deals, the more successful companies gained significant advantage along all of the performance axes. The less successful companies may have overestimated their market size and overstaffed their management teams.

  - Of the three industries in this category, dot-coms had the highest level of investor involvement at the seed stage, perhaps suggesting the influence of investors who had actually founded new dot-coms.

Key Findings: Market Conditions

The Internet/NASDAQ bubble had a profound impact upon the companies in our sample. Companies that received financing in the bubble:

- attracted strong management teams at the seed stage;

- had made little customer and business-model progress by the A round of financing;

- received high levels of added value (nonfinancial assistance) from their investors, including assistance that went far beyond additional infusions of cash; and

- experienced down rounds in the later stages of financing.

Companies that received financing prior to the bubble:

- progressed more slowly, but had more customers by their A rounds of financing, and

- increased in value as a result of customer success.

Key Findings: By Region

Our report examines both U.S. and European companies. Regional differences were strongly affected by industry. In comparing U.S. with non-U.S. companies:

- U.S. software companies in our sample developed strongly along the direct-sales customer axis. Non-U.S. companies developed more equally across the customer and channels axes, achieved stronger cash flow earlier, and made greater progress in product development.

- Measured as a group, the U.S. software, dot-com, and services companies we surveyed began with stronger management teams, investor contributions, and larger markets, and they achieved equal progress along the channels and customer axes as well as steady growth in customer acquisition. Non-U.S. firms performed better in terms of cash flow, saw more consistent progress along channels, and achieved better product development. By the B round, these companies had made more progress in channels, customers, business model, and cash flow than their U.S. counterparts.

- U.S. telecom and semiconductor companies had more participation from investors than non-U.S. firms and made steady progress along the customer acquisition axis. Non-U.S. firms focused more on channel development and cash flow management.

- European software companies tended to focus on channels, whereas U.S. firms were more concerned initially with direct sales.

- U.S. companies reported almost uniformly higher levels of lead investor assistance.

Key Findings: By Investor Role

Companies relied on their investors for a variety of nonfinancial services, particularly during the early stages of financing:

- During the period of our study, companies whose initial lead investors were venture capital firms tended to increase value less successfully than companies that received their initial round of financing from other sources. The reasons why are unclear. It may be that access to larger amounts of capital delayed the accomplishment of revenue, business model, and channels/alliances milestones.

- Companies backed by venture capitalists indicated higher levels of investor contribution during later rounds of financing. Such levels of involvement are typical of full-time, professional investors.

- Angel-backed companies gained substantial advantage along the channels/alliances and product development performance axes, while companies backed by venture capitalists focused more on customers.

- The most sought-after investor services were customer introductions and help in developing strategy and forming strategic alliances.

- Companies that chose venture capital firms as their lead investors traveled along different Paths to Value than did companies that chose angel investors; the former focused more on direct customer sales than on channels, and developed revenue later.

Conclusion: The Best Is Yet to Come

The Paths to Value model provides many insights into how early-stage ventures—in different industries and regions, operating under different market conditions—create value. However, this report is only the first. Much remains to be discovered and understood. The authors believe that the Paths to Value model may be able to generate a quantitative understanding of best practices for early-stage value creation. In this initial effort, our more modest goals are to provide insight into the factors that created value during a time of rapidly changing, tumultuous markets and to initiate a public dialog that could drive toward a consensus model for value creation. To stimulate such a dialog, we invite readers to visit our Paths to Value Web site at www. pathstovalue.com.

B. PATHS TO VALUE: INTRODUCTION

The economic events of the past three years have caused much soul-searching in the venture and entrepreneurial communities. While numerous, genuinely innovative companies achieved funding, so did many with business models best characterized as flimsy. During this period, investor sentiment swung from limitless confidence to paralyzing doubt. The vicissitudes of this tumultuous period did not result in a return to the pre-Internet world of the mid-nineties. But the bubble and the ensuing "bust" have fundamentally changed the venture-capital industry and forced a return to business basics.

More venture capital has been raised in the past three years than in the previous ten. Compared with four years ago, the average top-tier venture firm now manages more than three times more capital and must invest more per deal than ever before. This creates a fundamental challenge to the traditional venture capital business model. Early-stage capital, which flowed freely until mid 2000, has dried up, halting venture development at its source and forcing entrepreneurs to focus their efforts more than ever on critically important Paths to Value.

Entrepreneurs who launched startups during the recent boom are today forced to follow new models to help them build their next companies and to focus on specific strategic, execution, and resource criteria to create and sustain value in those new ventures. What lessons can be derived from the extremes of the boom and the bust? Will the renewed emphasis on business fundamentals transform the venture industry as completely as did the departure from fundamental principles? And what are the new prototypes that will foster early-stage value creation in these extraordinary times?

Paths to Value research and analysis trace the evolution of early-stage, VC-funded, high-tech firms that received funding during 1999, 2000, and 2001. In evaluating startup opportunities and value creation, most venture capitalists and observers of the early-stage market consider such factors as management experience, market opportunity, and competition. However, thus far, there has only been anecdotal reporting on the characteristics of these and other factors affecting value creation, on the different experiences of regions and industries, and on differing results due to market timing. This study uses an innovative approach—the Paths to Value model—to provide a new level of understanding and insight into the reasons why some firms increase in value while others do not.* It also represents a first step toward formalizing a new consensus model of value creation in early-stage ventures.

The Paths to Value Approach

In developing the Paths to Value approach, we surveyed executives at more than 350 U.S., European, and Israeli companies that received seed or first-round private equity financing in 1999, 2000, and 2001. These regions have the most active private equity markets in the world (see table on page 206). We surveyed companies in the biotech, telecommunications, semiconductor, software, and services industries. To make meaningful comparison possible, we sometimes grouped the R&D-intensive (biotech, semiconductor, and communications) and service-intensive (software and services) industries. We contrasted companies on the basis of degrees of success, as measured by value appreciation from initial to later financing rounds. We also selected companies that received financing prior to and during the bubble economy.

Survey questions were organized around three broad areas:

---

*As noted earlier, in time the Paths to Value approach may enable analysts to assess and predict firm value. That capability, however, is beyond the scope of this report.

strategy, resources, and performance. To each of these, we assigned three performance metrics, defined as "axes of value":

Macro Categories	Axes of Value
	Market Size
Strategy	Competitive Position
	Business Model
	Cash Flow
Resources	Investor Value Contributed
	Strength of Management Team
	Product Development
Performance	Channels/Alliances
	Customer Acquisition

The survey questions were intended to capture information related to the axes of value at each financing event. This approach enabled us to determine the steps taken by investors and management teams to increase value between rounds of financing (measured as a multiple of initial valuation). The data resulting from the responses to these questions were then plotted on Star Charts, described in detail below. Although we rated firms from 1 to 11 on each axis of value for each financing event, we found that, given the stage of development of these startups, the average score rarely exceeded 8. Therefore, the summary Star Charts in this document reflect axis scores from 0 to 8.*

Using this methodology, we were able to demonstrate the importance of regional distinctions, industry groupings, and market timing. While this approach yields many new and valuable insights into the early-stage value-creation process, it does not gen-

---

*For detailed descriptions of the axes and the meaning of a 1 score vis-à-vis a 10 score, see Appendix 4.

erate evidence that a single Path to Value exists. The timing and sequence of progress along any of the axes of value vary by industry, market environment, and many other factors. Hence, our insistence on the plural *Paths* to Value.

Developing the Model: What Entrepreneurs Need to Know

Entrepreneurs are interested in practical answers to such questions as these:

- When should I invest more in further developing my product?

- How and when should I engage sales channels?

- What level of customer traction justifies investment in ramping up sales?

- What should be the balance between growth and profitability?

- How developed were other companies in my industry when they successfully raised a particular round of financing?

However, to create a model that can provide answers to these questions, we needed to consider a more general set of issues. Specifically, we asked ourselves:

- How might we develop a model to explain the fundamental venture development milestones along Paths to Value?

- Have these varied due to market conditions?

- Would any model be able to capture a startup's most critical issues by financing round and by industry?

- Do venture development milestones in the United States differ from those in Europe? If so, what are the differences?

- Would any model be able to link a venture capital firm's hands-on involvement to the ultimate success of a portfolio company in the United States and in Europe?

- Did the boom and bust make that much difference? If so, to whom?

The Star Diagram: Visualizing the Paths to Value

To facilitate analysis, we adopted the use of Star Charts. These radar diagrams capture the course of a company's development at various stages. Each distinctively shaded layer of the Star Chart represents a point in time—for purposes of this report, a financing round. As noted earlier, three macrocategories on the chart encompass the strategy, resources, and performance of the companies depicted. Within each macrocategory are three specific performance metrics for a total of nine axes of value (see the table on page 206). Star Chart B-1 is a typical example:

Star Chart B-1: Typical Star Chart

Source: PricewaterhouseCoopers

Star Charts that illustrate a single startup may be interesting to the company in question, but offer no larger insights. However, Star Charts that capture a group of companies present a bigger picture, making analytical generalizations possible. All generalizations are hazardous—the details never seem to conform perfectly to the ideal case. Nevertheless, the aggregate comparisons made possible by Star Charts result in interesting conclusions about how value was added in a variety of market environments, industries, and regions of the world.

Understanding the Axes of Value

The axes of value are based on previous research in the early-stage venture market and on the modeling efforts and experience of the authors. In selecting the axes of value, we used the following criteria. As a group, the axes had to:

- Elicit objective answers, not just the respondent's opinions.

- Be robust and distinct—that is, plentiful enough to show differentiation, but not so numerous as to be unwieldy or in part superfluous.

- Approximate the decision-making criteria of early-stage investors.

- Be relevant to many industries, but also to various aspects of different industries.

- Span the life cycle of the companies studied.

Strategy: Market Size, Competitive Position, Business Model

The three axes located at the top and upper-right portion of the Star Chart relate to a company's *strategic* (external) situation. Market size (and readiness) is important because it represents a cap on potential sales volume. Competitive position can be protected by patents or other types of temporary monopoly and will dictate the company's ability to add value for investors. The business model measures the company's ability to articulate a pricing model that will eventually take advantage of positive economies of scale.

Resources: Cash Flow, Investor Value Contributed, Strength of Management Team

The three axes located on the lower portion of the diagram relate to the *resources* available to the company. Although many early-stage companies have not yet achieved cash flow break-even, revenues are an important indicator of the company's potential to fill a market niche. Evidence indicates that investors in the private equity market do more than write checks: they add value through services and advice. The strength of the management team is often a key determinant of success.

Performance: Product Development, Channels/Alliances, Customer Acquisition

The three axes located on the left portion of the diagram relate to important measures of company *performance*. The product development metric measures a company's progress in developing a working version of its good or service. The channels/alliances metric flows logically from product development—even the best product in the world will not sell if it is not distributed to its potential market. And finally, distribution is meaningless unless the company has been able to attract paying customers that can generate additional sales.

Reading a Star Chart

The Star Chart models a company's progress along each axis of value at each financing event. Each shaded polygon represents a company's status at a given point in time. Companies receive initial funding in a seed round. Subsequent financing rounds are labeled A, B, C, and D. Changes from round to round are captured by graphic depictions of execution milestones and each company's status with respect to these milestones. Because they aggregate data related to industry, financing round, market condition, country/region, and other factors, Star Charts also illustrate execution norms by industry segment and summarize factors that most closely correlate with success and value creation.

Star Charts B-2 and B-3 illustrate companies that chose different but successful Paths to Value. Star Chart B-2 represents a ser-

Star Chart B-2: Successful IPO Path to Value for a Services Firm

Success - IPO

Total Exits	1
# of Bankruptcies	0
AverageExitVal	$795,905,380
number of firms =	1
number of observations =	23
SEED	$15,000,000
A	$105,000,000
B	#DIV/0!
C	#DIV/0!
D	#DIV/0!

Legend: D, C, B, A, SEED

Source: PricewaterhouseCoopers

Note: MS = market size; CP = competitive position; BM = business model; CF = cash flow; IV = investor value contributed; SM = strength of management team; PD = product development; CH = channel alliances; CU = customer acquisition

vices company from our sample, which experienced a successful IPO. As the Star Chart indicates, even during early rounds of financing the company had progressed quite far along the product development, market size, and management strength value axes, and maintained that progress through later rounds. The company also was able to translate its progress on the performance axes into early cash flows. Star Chart B-3 illustrates companies that made successful exits through acquisition.

Star Chart B-3: Successful Acquisition Exits

Source: PricewaterhouseCoopers

Note: MS = market size; CP = competitive position; BM = business model; CF = cash flow; IV = investor value contributed; SM = strength of management team; PD = product development; CH = channel alliances; CU = customer acquisition

What Star Charts Illustrate

The Star Chart is a useful device for illustrating the patterns in company development, and also records one or several companies' progress along the nine axes of value. The axes are set on a scale that is developmentally appropriate to early-stage venture-backed companies. From round to round, successful companies will show steady progress on most of these value axes. However, declines along some axes over time do not always indicate erosion in value. Similarly, in some industries market size measurements may decline over time. This could result both from market timing and from the company's growing understanding of early opportunity in more focused market segments.

Each of the Star Charts above indicates significant progress on many axes from financing to financing. But the real power of the model lies in the distinctions it makes evident. For example, Star Chart B-2 (the IPO chart) illustrates a company that successfully built a channel, achieved good cash flow, and seized a strong competitive position very early. It also appeared to leverage these assets into significant customer acquisition over time. Star Chart B-3 (the acquisition chart), however, illustrates companies that had smaller markets and more gradual progress on all performance and strategy axes—leading, not surprisingly, to exits by acquisition rather than by IPO. The investors were also significantly involved in these later-stage companies and presumably played major roles in the acquisition deals.

What Star Charts Do Not Illustrate

Care must be exercised when interpreting multiple-company Star Charts because of the aggregation procedure underlying their creation. A Star Chart such as B-3, for example, indicates the average progress of a group of companies along the value axes over time. If a typical Star Chart includes thirty companies, the seed layer of the diagram would illustrate the average status of all thirty firms during the seed-financing event. However, readers should note that—unless otherwise specified—this seed event at the different companies is likely to have taken place at different times and that the composition of companies that form the layered polygons may change from round to round. Therefore, of the thirty companies depicted on a given Star Chart, perhaps twenty-five are included in the seed-round polygon, approximately thirty in the A round, a different group of twenty-five in the B round, and only twenty in the C round. Because our sample was selected from a pool of companies that underwent A round financing during our study period, more data generally exist on the earlier rounds. As well, some companies chose not to disclose information on their seed-round financing.

We do not present Star Charts that include all companies in the sample. Since each company is measured in a consistent way regardless of industry, interpreting Star Charts that include firms from different industry groups is somewhat problematic. For example, at any given round of financing, human resources-intensive companies are likely to be farther along in product development than capital-intensive companies. For this reason, wherever possible we examine subsamples of our data set by looking at companies grouped by industry. The Star Charts we present in this report view companies with key issues in common.

Different Circumstances, Different Paths

A central point of this report is that no single Path to Value exists. Performance along any of the nine axes of value will depend upon various factors. Given the composition of our sample companies, we were able to examine several variations of the Path to Value based on industry, market environment, region, and initial lead investor.

Industry Groups

One of our assumptions before the survey process began was that startup companies in different industries would share certain industry-specific characteristics. For this reason, we surveyed companies in a variety of industries. However, for the sake of analysis, we sometimes grouped companies together. For example, at times we combined R&D-intensive companies with pure technology development efforts and compared these with service-intensive companies. At other times, we split them apart. We analyzed a number of dot-com companies both as a separate group and also as software or services companies, according to how they characterized themselves.

Not unexpectedly, we found that firms in different industries develop along different paths. Section C of this book examines in detail the different Paths to Value taken by companies grouped by industry.

Market Environment

A part of this report focuses on the effect of the so-called Internet bubble—the significant increase in initial public offerings, Nasdaq valuations, and other activity related to the dot-com boom of late 1999 and early 2000. To account for the effects of this dynamic market environment, we divided our sample into four time periods:

Prebubble: First quarter 1998 to third quarter 1999
Bubble: Fourth quarter 1999 to second quarter 2000
Postbubble: Third quarter 2000 to first quarter 2001
Recession/Recovery: From second quarter 2001

To compare successful to unsuccessful ventures, we calculated Nasdaq-corrected amounts for reported valuations and amounts raised in financings. This enabled us to look across time periods at industry- and region-specific Paths to Value.

Figure B-1 indicates month-end average values of the Nasdaq stock exchange during the period of our study. The shaded areas indicate the time periods defined for this study.

Appendices

Figure B-1: Month-End Average Values of Nasdaq

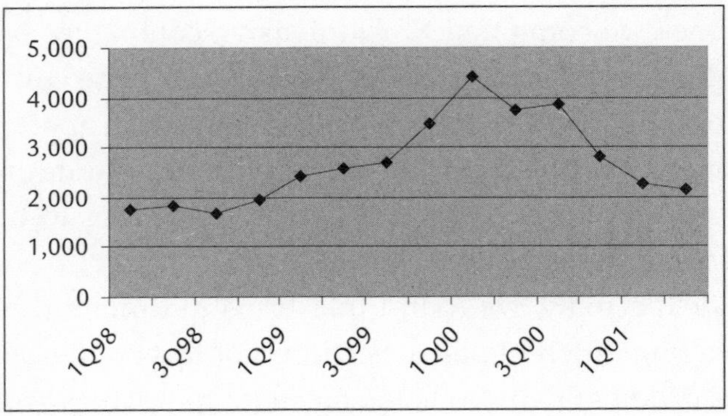

Source: PricewaterhouseCoopers

Section D of this book examines the implications of market environment.

Region

Our sample was almost evenly divided between U.S. companies and companies operating in major venture capital markets outside the United States—specifically in the United Kingdom, other parts of Western Europe, and Israel. We surveyed ventures across all industry groups in all regions. In so doing, we discovered the importance of tracking region-related Paths to Value in terms of one industry group at a time.

As Figures B-2 indicates, the countries included in our survey accounted for the vast majority of technology investment during the year 2000, the latest year for which estimated figures are available. The United States had the largest amount, followed by countries in Western Europe. We also surveyed some companies located in Israel, which accounted for the vast majority of investment in the Middle East and Africa.

Figure B-2: Global Technology Private Equity Investment 2000

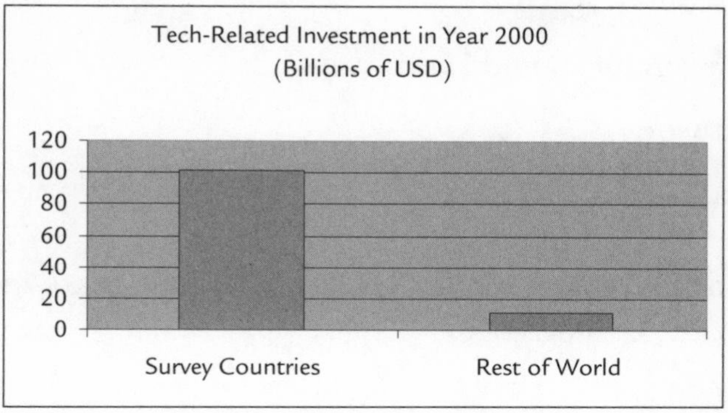

Tech-Related Investment in Year 2000
(Billions of USD)

Source: PwC and 3i, Global Private Equity 200

Section E of this report discusses the insights and Paths to Value that emerged from our regional analysis.

Role of the Investor

In addition to looking at industry, market environment, and region, we also came to some interesting conclusions as to how the investor affects value creation. These relate to the initial lead investor (defined as the investor who contributes at least 50 percent of the seed or A round investment), to the continuing service functions provided by investors as the companies mature, and to differing Star Chart patterns in light of the role of investors at successive rounds of financing. We also examined the degree of satisfaction with their investors among managers of startups. Section F discusses these findings.

C. INDUSTRY DESCRIPTIONS AND COMPARISONS

In analyzing Paths to Value by industry, we selected industry segments that historically have attracted the vast majority of venture financing over the last five years:

- Biotech

- Telecom

- Semiconductor and Hardware

- Software

- Services

We further refined our analysis by grouping these industries into two major categories:

- *R&D-oriented industries:* Telecom and Semiconductor (and in some comparisons Biotech as well)—Companies operating in these industries are physical capital-intensive and are involved in the development of fundamental technologies.

- *Service-oriented industries:* Software and Services— Companies operating in these industries are human capital-intensive.

In addition, for some comparisons we isolated dot-com ventures. The dot-com industry segment often contained an implicit business-to-consumer (B2C) strategy that had fallen out of fashion by the time we conducted this survey. Those dot-com companies that still existed during our survey period categorized themselves as either services or software, depending on the products they were offering (or planning to offer) at the time of the survey. Because of the volatile nature of sentiment concerning the dot-com industry segment, we examined some industry characteristics independently. For example, some Star Charts refer only to companies with dot-com in their names. At other times, as appropriate, we included dot-com companies in their self-selected industry groups (software or services).

Chart C-1 illustrates the industry breakdown used in this portion of our study. In this chart, dot-com companies are categorized either as software or as services, depending on their self-selected industry designation.

Chart C-1: Breakdown of Industry Groups

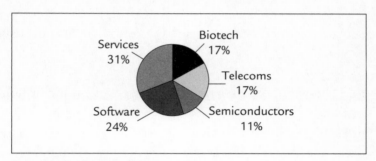

Source: PricewaterhouseCoopers

Chart C-2 illustrates the average success ratio by industry. In preparing this chart, we used a ratio based on the most recently reported valuation data divided by initial reported valuation amount. In other words, the chart measures total value added less any additional capital raised, divided by the original premoney valuation.* Because startup companies are not publicly traded, the success ratios approximate value appreciation based on interim valuations, that is, the change in valuation between different financing events. The success number indicates *actual* final value added only for companies that had an actual exit event (an acquisition, bankruptcy, or IPO).

---

*The actual equation is as follows. Final pre + last amount raised – initial pre – total amount raised)/initial pre.

Chart C-2: Average Success Ratio by Industry

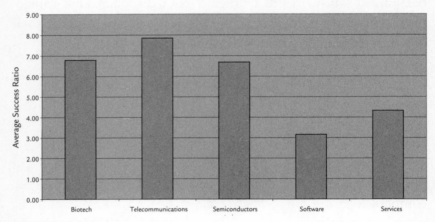

Source: PricewaterhouseCoopers

Industry Star Charts

For our industry analysis, we sought the most representative re-sults. Because of the common characteristics shared by companies in each grouping, we combined R&D-intensive companies (tele-com and semiconductor) and compared them to service-intensive companies (software and services). Because of inadequate sample size, we excluded biotech companies in the following analysis.

R&D-Intensive Industries—Telecom and Semiconductor

As Star Charts C-1 and C-2 indicate, the successful companies in this category began life with a more developed business model than the less successful firms, perhaps indicating a better early understanding of the economic value of their products. The successful companies also showed steady progress along the customer acquisition axis, reflecting early cash flow that grew steadily over the course of financing events. With respect to prod-uct development, successful companies in this industry category started slowly, but accelerated at a steady pace. The unsuccessful companies started out with better initial product development (perhaps indicating premature levels of commitment to one type of product, or what is commonly referred to as a "technology-driven" approach as opposed to "market or customer-driven").

One interesting finding from this analysis is that unsuccessful companies in our sample raised their seed financing at higher valuations. At this milestone, they were farther along than successful companies on the product development axis and perceived themselves to be in stronger initial competitive positions. However, at the same milestone—the seed financing round—the successful companies had identified larger markets, and by later financing rounds had moved ahead of the less successful companies on most measurements.

Star Chart C-1: Successful R&D-Intensive Firms*

iround# = <4, SuccValAddCorr>1ValObs = >3, ind.tel.semi = 2.5, all = all

Total Exits	1
# of Bankruptcies	0
AverageExitVal	$100,087,866
number of firms =	14
number of observations =	406
SEED	$2,978,750
A	$9,457,640
B	$58,030,750
C	$149,407,143
D	#DIV/0!

Legend: SEED, A, B, C, D

Source: PricewaterhouseCoopers

Note: MS = market size; CP = competitive position; BM = business model; CF = cash flow; IV = investor value contributed; SM = strength of management team; PD = product development; CH = channel alliances; CU = customer acquisition

*Excluding biotech due to small sample size.

Star Chart C-2: Less Successful R&D-Intensive Firms*

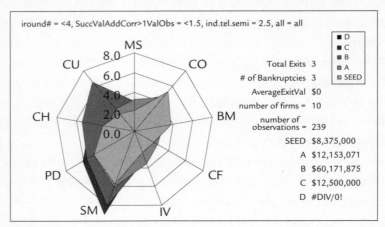

iround# = <4, SuccValAddCorr>1ValObs = <1.5, ind.tel.semi = 2.5, all = all

Total Exits	3	
# of Bankruptcies	3	
AverageExitVal	$0	
number of firms =	10	
number of observations =	239	
SEED	$8,375,000	
A	$12,153,071	
B	$60,171,875	
C	$12,500,000	
D	#DIV/0!	

Source: PricewaterhouseCoopers

Note: MS = market size; CP = competitive position; BM = business model; CF = cash flow; IV = investor value contributed; SM = strength of management team; PD = product development; CH = channel alliances; CU = customer acquisition

*Excluding biotech due to small sample size.

Perhaps the most important difference between successful and unsuccessful companies in this category is that the more successful firms had higher levels of investor assistance (investor value contributed) and that these levels increased steadily at each round of financing. Successful firms in this industry segment tended to establish a limited set of major strategic customer and original equipment manufacturer (OEM) deals, in which experienced investors played an important role.

Service-Intensive Industries: Software, Services, and Dot-Com

Determining startups' proper peer groups is one issue that complicates the effort to identify Paths to Value. In order to maximize the potential for insights from our sample of companies, we divided the companies into two major industry categories: service-intensive and R&D-intensive. What service-intensive companies have in common is that they rely much less on physical capital or manufacturing and have shorter product development life cycles. These shared characteristics enabled us to examine as a group their progress along the nine axes of value. However, since some differences may exist between the Paths to Value for services as opposed to those of software companies, we also performed some industry-specific comparisons.

We discovered that among companies operating in service-intensive industries, degrees of success were more finely shaded than among R&D-intensive firms. For this reason, in our analysis we discuss those companies as being either "highly successful," "most successful," "less successful," or "least successful" with respect to their industry category.

Finally, our research included a handful of service-intensive companies that raised $20 million or more by the end of the survey period—far more than the majority of companies surveyed. We discuss some of the implications of this disparity.

Software, Services, Dot-Coms

At the seed stage, the most successful companies in this combined category showed higher scores on all value axes but two: market size and strength of management team. These two were significantly higher for the less successful companies. Among startups that acquired initial beta customers and negotiated channel deals, the more successful companies had significant advantages along all performance axes. The less successful companies perhaps overestimated their market size and might have overstaffed and accelerated their burn rates ahead of opportunity.

By the B round of financing, the more successful companies were showing significant progress along all performance axes and were ramping up cash flow with significant revenue. At the same time, the less successful companies had little channel activity, modest customer acquisition progress, and little revenue.

Interestingly, by the C round, the less successful companies were reporting larger target markets and stronger competitive positions than their more successful counterparts, but had made little progress on revenue or business models. Their opportunity appears to have been more speculative than actual, especially when one considers that the more successful companies had valuations nearly twice as high as the less successful firms at this financing round.

Most striking, however, is the strong correlation among these companies between customer acquisition and cash flow. Even as early as the A round of financing, the more successful companies were achieving high cash flow scores. They were earning revenues while keeping expenses down and were at or close to break-even by the later rounds. In other words, they were raising capital to accelerate growth rather than to meet expenses.

Star Charts C-3 and C-4 illustrate these findings.

Finally, our sample of ventures in this industry grouping contained a small sample of eight companies that raised more than $20 million. By contrast, our survey included more than 150 companies in these industries that raised less than $20 million by the end of the survey period. As Star Charts C-5 and C-6 make clear, the differences between the companies in these two groups are less about success and more about choices concerning Paths to Value.

Taken together, the eight companies that raised more than $20 million had an average, Nasdaq-corrected premoney valuation of $14.6 million in their initial round. These large initial valuations may suggest the significant impact of market timing. By the A round, these companies had achieved high scores on the strategy, investor, and management team value axes. During the same period, companies raising smaller amounts focused on customer

Star Chart C-3: Most Successful Software, Services, and Dot-Com Companies

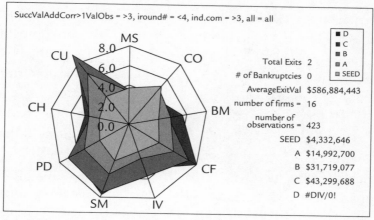

SuccValAddCorr>1ValObs = >3, iround# = <4, ind.com = >3, all = all

Total Exits 2
# of Bankruptcies 0
AverageExitVal $586,884,443
number of firms = 16
number of observations = 423
SEED $4,332,646
A $14,992,700
B $31,719,077
C $43,299,688
D #DIV/0!

Source: PricewaterhouseCoopers

Star Chart C-4: Least Successful Software, Services, and Dot-Com Companies

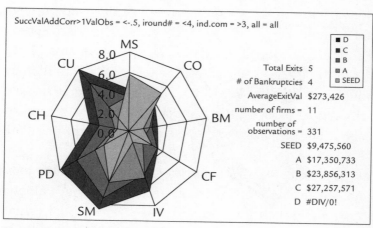

SuccValAddCorr>1ValObs = <-.5, iround# = <4, ind.com = >3, all = all

Total Exits 5
# of Bankruptcies 4
AverageExitVal $273,426
number of firms = 11
number of observations = 331
SEED $9,475,560
A $17,350,733
B $23,856,313
C $27,257,571
D #DIV/0!

Source: PricewaterhouseCoopers

Note: MS = market size; CP = competitive position; BM = business model; CF = cash flow; IV = investor value contributed; SM = strength of management team; PD = product development; CH = channel alliances; CU = customer acquisition

Star Chart C-5: Software, Services, and Dot-Com Companies— Raised More Than $20 Million

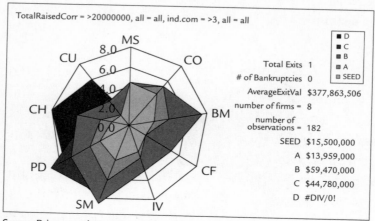

Source: PricewaterhouseCoopers

Star Chart C-6: Software, Services, and Dot-Com Companies— Raised Less Than $20 Million

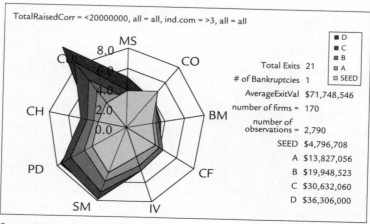

Source: PricewaterhouseCoopers

Note: MS = market size; CP = competitive position; BM = business model; CF = cash flow; IV = investor value contributed; SM = strength of management team; PD = product development; CH = channel alliances; CU = customer acquisition

cash flow and on early success along the three performance axes. By the B round, access to additional capital had moved the companies raising more money into higher scores along all axes, indicating a significant scaling up of their ventures.

Software

When compared to the service-oriented companies as a group, successful software companies performed consistently better across the board on the customers, channels, and product development value axes.

As Star Charts C-7 and C-8 reveal, across all rounds of financing the most successful software companies demonstrated a balance between channels and direct sales to customers. In contrast, less successful software companies, particularly in the early rounds, made little progress on their channel strategy. Since many software companies sell products through alliance partners that provide critical related services, this distinction may have had a major impact on early value.

Consistent with their channel strategy, the most successful software companies also paid more attention than their less successful counterparts to growing revenue and to building a scalable business model. They also made greater and steadier progress on product development.

In our sample, the group of less successful software companies included several that filed for bankruptcy. Quite early these companies focused on what they perceived (or hoped) to be very large markets. As a result of what could have been a misperception, these companies never reached sufficient customer, revenue, and business model traction, and perhaps did not refocus quickly enough on smaller market niches where they might have been able to establish competitive barriers and possibly succeed.

Star Chart C-7: Most Successful Software

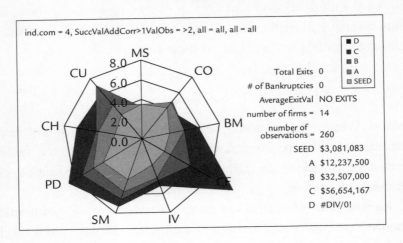

Source: PricewaterhouseCoopers

Star Chart C-8: Less Successful Software

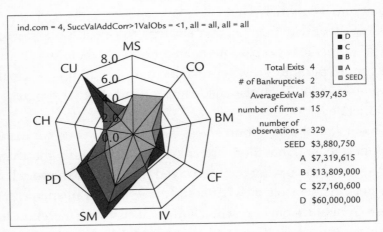

Source: PricewaterhouseCoopers

Note: MS = market size; CP = competitive position; BM = business model; CF = cash flow; IV = investor value contributed; SM = strength of management team; PD = product development; CH = channel alliances; CU = customer acquisition

Services

Star Charts C-9 and C-10 indicate that the most successful services companies did a much better job of selling directly to customers than less successful companies, which attempted to bridge the gap by accelerating their channel strategy in the B round of financing. It is significant to note that for these companies, investor value contributed rose significantly during later rounds of financing, perhaps suggesting an attempt on the part of investors to save them. Conversely, successful companies show investor involvement earlier rather than later.

With respect to markets, the more successful services companies focused on narrow markets early, avoiding the misperceptions about market size that plagued their less successful competitors.

Star Chart C-9: Most Successful Services

ind.com = 5, iround# = <5, SuccValAddCorr>1ValObs = >1, all = all

Total Exits	1
# of Bankruptcies	0
AverageExitVal	$795,905,380
number of firms =	17
number of observations =	369
SEED	$5,883,500
A	$16,441,353
B	$21,165,071
C	$37,405,833
D	$10,000,000

Source: PricewaterhouseCoopers

Note: MS = market size; CP = competitive position; BM = business model; CF = cash flow; IV = investor value contributed; SM = strength of management team; PD = product development; CH = channel alliances; CU = customer acquisition

Star Chart C-10: Less Successful Services

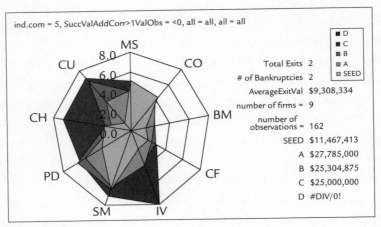

Source: PricewaterhouseCoopers

Note: MS = market size; CP = competitive position; BM = business model; CF = cash flow; IV = investor value contributed; SM = strength of management team; PD = product development; CH = channel alliances; CU = customer acquisition

Successful companies also were more driven by markets (channels and customers) and by technology (product development).

Finally, market timing had a huge impact on the services sector. The most successful services companies were founded at lower seed and A round valuations, indicating that they received early financing before the bubble. Less successful companies, however, were founded at the higher valuations typical of companies that received early financing during the bubble. These companies were able to attract strong management teams from the outset, but suffered as market conditions changed and found themselves incapable of increasing their market-corrected valuations.

Conclusion: Key Findings

A number of important differences—some of them counterintuitive—emerged by industry:

- General

  - The importance of early-customer revenue differed dramatically among the industry groups studied. Early and consistently growing revenue was critical to services and software companies. Biotech companies had little revenue during an extended R&D period. And telecom and semiconductor companies sometimes acquired beta and test customers that produced little revenue.

  - Industry characteristics determined the degree of emphasis placed by an early-stage company on its technology, channels, and customers.

- Telecom and Semiconductor

  - The most successful firms raised their seed financing with larger identified markets and benefited from high levels of steadily increasing value.

  - Less successful firms raised their seed financing at higher valuations and emphasized well-developed products and strong early competitive positions. At initial financing, these companies were farther along than successful companies on the product development axis, and perceived themselves to be in stronger initial competitive positions. By later financing rounds, the more successful companies had moved ahead of their less successful counterparts on most measurements.

  - Firms that were more successful availed themselves of higher levels of investor assistance, and these levels increased steadily at each round of financing.

- Software

  - The more successful firms as a whole demonstrated a balance between channels and direct sales approaches.

- The less successful firms had weak channel strategies.

- The most successful companies paid more attention than their less successful counterparts to growing revenue and building a scalable business model. These companies also made greater and steadier progress on the product development value axis.

- A more developed product is not always better. A large number of the failed software companies achieved significant product development as they burned through investment dollars without achieving robust progress in customer acquisition and cash flow.

- Services

  - The more successful firms exploited direct sales, focused early on narrow markets, were driven by markets (customers and channels) rather than technology, and experienced low seed and A round valuations.

  - The less successful firms had less success with direct sales, tended to focus on broader markets, were driven by technology, and were founded at higher valuations.

- Dot-Coms, Services, and Software Combined

  - Successful firms showed strong cash flow and scored high on all value axes.

  - At the seed stage, the most successful companies scored higher on all value axes but two: market size and strength of management team. The less successful companies excelled along these value axes. Among startups that acquired initial beta customers and negotiated channel deals, the more successful companies gained significant advantage along all of the performance axes. The less successful companies perhaps overestimated their market size and overstaffed their management teams.

- Of the three industries in this category, dot-coms had the highest level of investor involvement at the seed stage, perhaps suggesting the influence of investors that had actually founded new dot-coms.

Needless to say, an entirely different set of distinctions surfaced when we applied the Paths to Value model to market environment.

D. MARKET ENVIRONMENT

At the peak of the Internet mania, "dot-com" rather than "quality business plan" were the magic words to attract funding. However, during the bust that followed and the subsequent recession and recovery, the pendulum swung in the other direction, with industry participants complaining that even solid startup businesses could not acquire the funding they needed. This section examines the effect of the Internet bubble on the valuation and performance of high-tech startup firms in the software and services industry segment.

Among the sample companies and during the period of our study, the Internet bubble had the greatest effect on the valuations of service-intensive companies. Many of the R&D-intensive companies in the telecom and semiconductor markets experienced similar market fluctuations, but these occurred slightly later. Because we measured ventures only at times of new investments, we captured little postbubble information on these companies. For this reason, this section of our report focuses primarily on companies in the service-intensive category.

We first isolated the dot-com companies for analysis.* Next, we examined all service-intensive companies that received their A round of financing during the bubble and compare the Star Charts for firms that went on to succeed against those for firms that were not as successful.

Last, we broke out services firms (our sample contains many) and compared successful companies that received their A round of financing during the bubble to those that received it before the bubble. This comparison allowed us to compare the ingredients of success as they were before the bubble with those at work during the bubble.

In order to account for the effects of the dynamic market environment in the service-intensive industries, we divided our sample into four time periods:

Prebubble: First quarter 1998 to third quarter 1999
Bubble: Fourth quarter 1999 to second quarter 2000
Postbubble: Third quarter 2000 to first quarter 2001
Recession/Recovery: From second quarter 2001 to 2003

Doing Business in and Around the Bubble

While many companies created during this period eventually failed, many others succeeded. The bubble drove up valuations, but it also affected and was driven by capital spending in the IT sector. Because corporations were spending large amounts of money on products and services related to information technology, the effect of the bubble is evident not only in inflated valuations and amounts raised but also in cash flow infusions based on sales.

Figure D-1 indicates the amounts raised by all firms in our

---

*See the discussions on industry groups, above, for the reasons why dot.com companies represent a sub-sample from which interesting lessons can be drawn.

Figure D-1: Total Amount Raised Versus Nasdaq

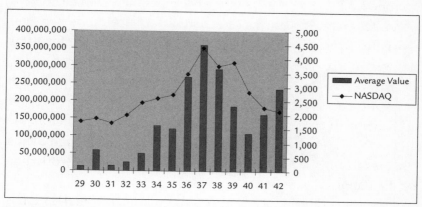

Source: PricewaterhouseCoopers

sample. The chart shows that inflows into early-stage companies were highly correlated to the ebb and flow of Nasdaq total market capitalization from 1998 to 2001.

Dot-Com Survivors

Many dot-coms became "dot-bombs." In our study, we discovered some interesting reasons why the survivors were able to avoid bankruptcy. One key reason is that dot-com companies that survived the bubble had a great deal of help. As Star Chart D-1 indicates, investors were deeply involved in these companies during their seed stages. This involvement, however, decreased as the companies built their management teams.

Other factors that may have contributed to the success of these companies include the following:

- They spent liberally to attract strong and complete management teams at early financing stages.

Star Chart D-1: Dot-Com Survivors

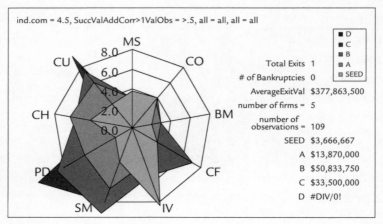

ind.com = 4.5, SuccValAddCorr>1ValObs = >.5, all = all, all = all

Total Exits	1
# of Bankruptcies	0
AverageExitVal	$377,863,500
number of firms =	5
number of observations =	109
SEED	$3,666,667
A	$13,870,000
B	$50,833,750
C	$33,500,000
D	#DIV/0!

Source: PricewaterhouseCoopers

Note: MS = market size; CP = competitive position; BM = business model; CF = cash flow; IV = investor value contributed; SM = strength of management team; PD = product development; CH = channel alliances; CU = customer acquisition

- Product development reached maturity quickly, as one might expect when the product is a hosted Internet service rather than a physical object that must be manufactured, packaged, and shipped.*

Interestingly, while most of these companies acquired respectable customer bases, few made significant progress on their business models, indicating the lack among them of pricing models that could have led to increased growth and profitability.

---

*This finding reinforced the logic of separating out the services-oriented firms from the R&D-oriented firms, as we have done throughout this report.

Inside the Bubble: Dot-Com, Software, and Services

Moving from dot-coms to a wider view of service-intensive companies, we discovered that successful ventures that received their A round of financing in the bubble were more market focused than unsuccessful companies. Their customer acquisition and channels/alliances scores were higher, and continued at higher levels throughout subsequent financing rounds.

In addition, the more successful companies not only scored higher in the cash flow (revenue/expenses) metric during later rounds of financing but also in their earlier stages of development and in relation to their customer acquisition scores. As Star Charts D-2 and D-3 indicate, the more successful companies were able to

Star Chart D-2: Successful Dot-Com, Software, and Services with A Round During Bubble

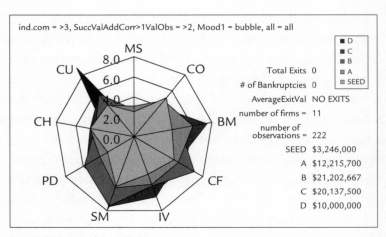

Source: PricewaterhouseCoopers

Note: MS = market size; CP = competitive position; BM = business model; CF = cash flow; IV = investor value contributed; SM = strength of management team; PD = product development; CH = channel alliances; CU = customer acquisition

Star Chart D-3: Unsuccessful Dot-Com, Software, and Services with A Round During Bubble

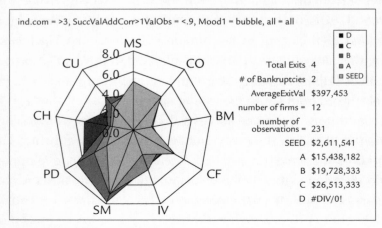

ind.com = >3, SuccValAddCorr>1ValObs = <.9, Mood1 = bubble, all = all

Total Exits	4
# of Bankruptcies	2
AverageExitVal	$397,453
number of firms =	12
number of observations =	231
SEED	$2,611,541
A	$15,438,182
B	$19,728,333
C	$26,513,333
D	#DIV/0!

Source: PricewaterhouseCoopers

Note: MS = market size; CP = competitive position; BM = business model; CF = cash flow; IV = investor value contributed; SM = strength of management team; PD = product development; CH = channel alliances; CU = customer acquisition

achieve a cash flow score of 5.2 and a customer acquisition score of 4.1 in their A round. Less successful companies, however, were only at 3.8 and 4.4, respectively, for cash flow and customer acquisition by their B rounds. This high expense ratio could be related to a larger staff—less successful companies acquired higher-level management teams earlier than successful companies.

Successful and unsuccessful companies moved in tandem along the product development, channels/alliances, and customer acquisition value axes. However, less successful companies appear to have emphasized product development at the expense of customer engagement. Successful companies also seemed better able to appraise the size of their markets realistically and conservatively.

Inside and Outside the Bubble: Services

In the bubble, many companies were able to attract strong management teams at the seed stage, and services companies were no exception. It is also apparent from Star Charts D-4 and D-5 that in the bubble investors focused on providing significant value, taking an active role to accelerate their companies.

Before the bubble, services companies grew over a longer period of time and were farther along the customer acquisition value axis prior to raising financing during an A round at a much higher average valuation.

While some companies that began life in the bubble did succeed, on average they still experienced down rounds in the later stages. However, companies that received their A round before

Star Chart D-4: Successful Services—Received A Round During Bubble

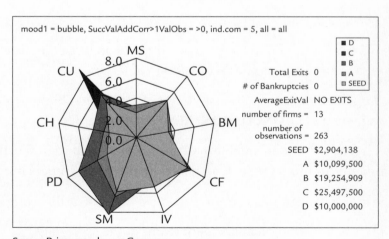

mood1 = bubble, SuccValAddCorr>1ValObs = >0, ind.com = 5, all = all

Total Exits	0
# of Bankruptcies	0
AverageExitVal	NO EXITS
number of firms =	13
number of observations =	263
SEED	$2,904,138
A	$10,099,500
B	$19,254,909
C	$25,497,500
D	$10,000,000

Source: PricewaterhouseCoopers

Note: MS = market size; CP = competitive position; BM = business model; CF = cash flow; IV = investor value contributed; SM = strength of management team; PD = product development; CH = channel alliances; CU = customer acquisition

Star Chart D-5: Successful Services—Received A Round Before the Bubble

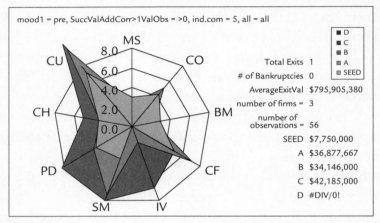

Source: PricewaterhouseCoopers

Note: MS = market size; CP = competitive position; BM = business model; CF = cash flow; IV = investor value contributed; SM = strength of management team; PD = product development; CH = channel alliances; CU = customer acquisition

the bubble continued to increase in value due in large measure to success along the customer acquisition value axis.

CONCLUSION: KEY FINDINGS

The Internet/Nasdaq bubble had a profound impact upon the companies in our sample. Companies that received financing in the bubble:

- attracted strong management teams at the seed stage;

- had made little customer and business model progress by the A round of financing;

- received high levels of added value (nonfinancial assistance) from their investors; and

- experienced down rounds in the later stages of financing.

Companies that received financing prior to the bubble:

- progressed more slowly, but had more customers by their A round of financing; and

- increased in value as a result of ongoing customer success.

E. REGIONAL ASPECTS OF EARLY-STAGE FINANCING

Because our sample contained both U.S. and non-U.S. companies, we were able to compare the value-creation process in the United States to that in Europe, including the United Kingdom. Figure E-1 illustrates the breakdown of companies in our sample based on their self-reported locations.

We performed a number of comparisons to determine how the Paths to Value varied by geographical region. However, as al-

Figure E-1: Firms Located in Regions

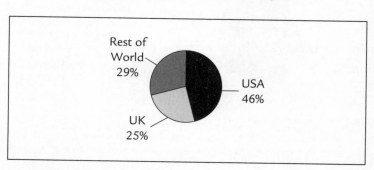

Source: PricewaterhouseCoopers

ready noted, industry differences can have a profound impact. Therefore, while we examine a number of regional differences in this section, we do so in the context of the two major industry categories on which we have focused throughout this report: companies that are R&D-intensive (telecom and semiconductor) and those that are service-intensive (software, services, dot-coms).

Regional Differences by Industry

R&D-Intensive Industries: Telecoms and Semiconductors

As Star Charts E-1 and E-2 illustrate, when compared to their European counterparts, U.S.-based telecom and semiconductor companies experienced higher levels of investor participation that increased over time in proportion with progress along the cus-

Star Chart E-1: U.S. Successful Telecom and Semiconductor Firms

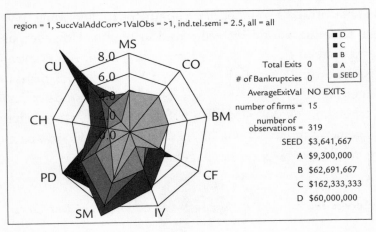

Source: PricewaterhouseCoopers

Note: MS = market size; CP = competitive position; BM = business model; CF = cash flow; IV = investor value contributed; SM = strength of management team; PD = product development; CH = channel alliances; CU = customer acquisition

Star Chart E-2: Non-U.S. Successful Telecom and Semiconductor Firms

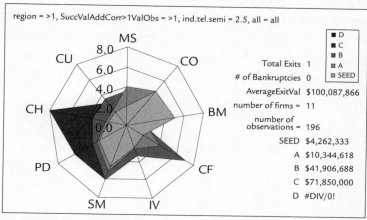

Source: PricewaterhouseCoopers

Note: MS = market size; CP = competitive position; BM = business model; CF = cash flow; IV = investor value contributed; SM = strength of management team; PD = product development; CH = channel alliances; CU = customer acquisition

tomer acquisition value axis. In addition, while U.S. companies exhibited steady progress along this axis, European companies focused more on channel development. Moreover, U.S. firms built stronger management teams, especially in later rounds of financing, while non-U.S. companies made better progress on cash flow management, reflecting both higher revenues and, perhaps more important, better expense management.

Service-Intensive Industries: Software, Services, and Dot-Coms

As previously noted, companies within this group share certain characteristics. Key among them is that they typically do not have many millions of dollars and many years of technology development behind them before they begin to acquire customers and generate revenue. We did, however, uncover some important regional differences.

For example, U.S. firms in our sample started out with stronger management teams and experienced steady growth in customer acquisition. Non-U.S. firms that we surveyed performed better in terms of cash flow, progressed more consistently along the channels/alliances value axis, and achieved better product development.

Software: Same Success, Different Paths

Because software companies form one of the larger industry groups in our sample, we were able to compare industry-specific U.S. and non-U.S. data. Although the companies included in Star Charts E-3 and E-4 successfully provided added value to their in-

Star Chart E-3: Successful U.S. Software Firms

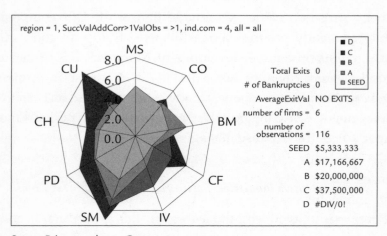

Source: PricewaterhouseCoopers

Note: MS = market size; CP = competitive position; BM = business model; CF = cash flow; IV = investor value contributed; SM = strength of management team; PD = product development; CH = channel alliances; CU = customer acquisition

Star Chart E-4: Successful Non-U.S. Software Firms

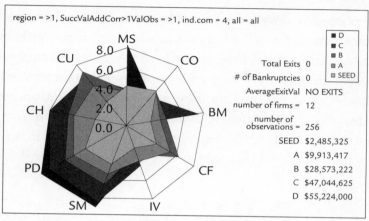

Source: PricewaterhouseCoopers

Note: MS = market size; CP = competitive position; BM = business model; CF = cash flow; IV = investor value contributed; SM = strength of management team; PD = product development; CH = channel alliances; CU = customer acquisition

vestors, they nevertheless displayed significantly different paths to value creation.

United States software companies performed more strongly in direct sales to customers, while non-U.S. companies split their focus between customers and channels. As a result, non-U.S. companies developed stronger cash flow earlier—as early as the seed round—and this led to the development of clearer business models. Their focus on channel strategy also resulted in lower expenses, further expediting improved cash flow. Non-U.S. firms also made better progress in product development, enabling them to manufacture and ship more and better products.

Regional Differences: Market Environment

The bubble economy in the United States had a global impact. But as Star Charts E-5 and E-6 indicate, regional differences clearly existed.* U.S. companies that received their A round financing during the bubble started out with stronger management teams, higher levels of investor contribution, larger markets, and even progress along both the channels/alliances and customer acquisition value axes. They also experienced steady growth in acquiring customers. Non-U.S. companies progressed more consistently

Star Chart E-5: U.S. Software, Dot-Com, and Services with A Round During Bubble

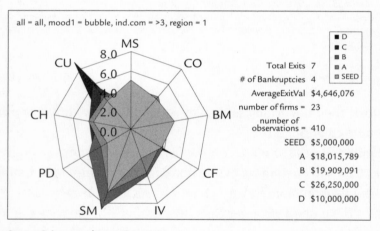

Source: PricewaterhouseCoopers

Note: MS = market size; CP = competitive position; BM = business model; CF = cash flow; IV = investor value contributed; SM = strength of management team; PD = product development; CH = channel alliances; CU = customer acquisition

---

*Rather than sort for success, these Star Charts combine both successes and failures. The U.S. sample includes twenty-three firms, of which four went bankrupt and three others had a positive exit. The non-U.S. sample consisted of forty-one companies, of which two went bankrupt and three had positive exits.

Star Chart E-6: Non-U.S. Software, Dot-Com, and Services with A Round During Bubble

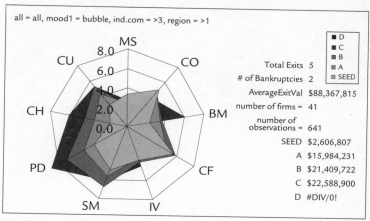

Source: PricewaterhouseCoopers

Note: MS = market size; CP = competitive position; BM = business model; CF = cash flow; IV = investor value contributed; SM = strength of management team; PD = product development; CH = channel alliances; CU = customer acquisition

along the channels/alliances axis and achieved better product development and higher levels of cash flow.

By the time these companies reached their B round of financing, non-U.S. firms had overtaken U.S. companies across a range of value axes, including channels/alliances, customer acquisition, business model, and cash flow. This may have been accomplished by targeting smaller, more focused market segments.

Regional Differences: Role of Investors

Figure E-2 indicates the level of services provided by lead investors. An interesting finding is that firms located in the United States reported almost uniformly higher levels of assistance from their lead investor.

Figure E-2: Services Provided by Lead Investor, by Region

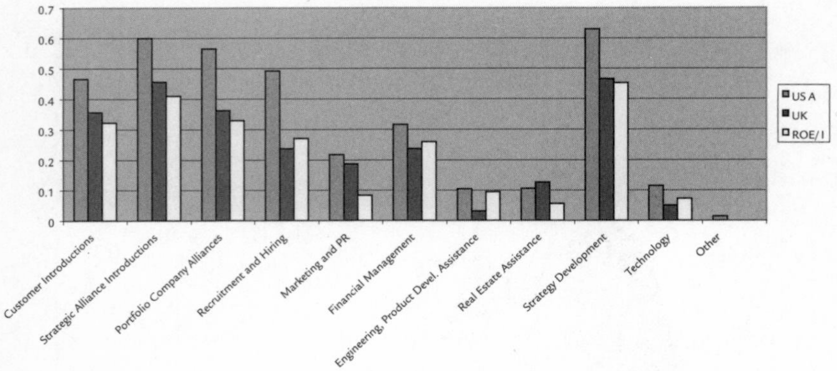

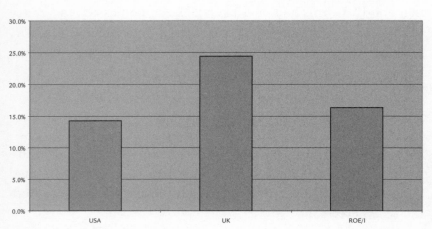

Source: PricewaterhouseCoopers

Figure E-3 indicates that managers of U.K. companies were least satisfied with their venture capital investors and were less likely than companies in the United States or continental Europe to seek out their current VCs in a capital-rich environment.

Figure E-3: Would Not Use Lead Investor Again, by Region

Source: PricewaterhouseCoopers

We shall have more to say about the role of the investor in the next section.

Conclusion: Key Findings

Regional differences were strongly affected by industry. In comparing U.S. with non-U.S. companies:

- United States software companies in our sample developed strongly along the direct sales customer axis. Non-U.S. companies developed more equally across the customer and channels axes, achieved stronger cash flow earlier, and made greater progress in product development.

- Measured as a group, the U.S. software, dot-com, and services companies surveyed began with stronger management teams, investor contributions, and larger markets, and they achieved equal progress along the channels and customer axes and steady growth in customer acquisition. Non-U.S. firms performed better in terms of cash flow, saw more consistent progress along channels, and achieved better product development. By the B round, these companies had made more progress in channels, customers, business model, and cash flow than their U.S. counterparts.

- U.S. telecom and semiconductor companies had more participation from investors than non-U.S. firms and made steady progress along the customer acquisition axis. Non-U.S. firms focused more on channel development and cash flow management.

- European software companies tended to focus on channels, whereas U.S. firms were more concerned initially with direct sales.

- U.S. companies reported almost uniformly higher levels of lead investor assistance.

F. ROLE OF INVESTOR

Our research confirmed that investors affect the Paths to Value. Although the majority of the companies in our sample received the bulk of their initial round of financing from venture capital firms, others turned to angels, corporate VCs, corporate investors, management-founders, and incubators. Figure F-1 provides a breakdown of our survey sample by lead investor.

As Figure F-2 clearly indicates, different lead investors performed different types of nonfinancial services for the firms in their portfolios. Not surprisingly, incubators were more likely to provide real estate assistance, although they were also tapped for nonpecuniary assistance (for example, help with approaching other investors). VCs were more likely to provide strategic assistance than were other types of lead investors. Corporate VC lead investors were most likely to offer help with engineering and product development. An interesting finding from these data is

Figure F-1: Initial Lead Investor

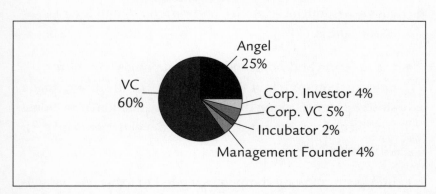

Source: PricewaterhouseCoopers

Figure F-2: Services Provided by Type of Lead Investor

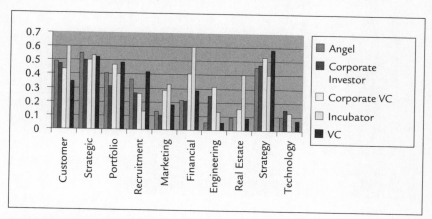

Source: PricewaterhouseCoopers

that angels were somewhat more likely than VC firms to provide customer introductions and to help form strategic alliances, although this finding varied widely from round to round and within industries and regions.

In our sample and throughout the time period under study, a correlation can be found between interim company success* and type of initial lead investor. Figure F-3 indicates the success ratio based on the initial lead investor.[†] Of the companies in our sample, those with VC lead investors tended to have smaller in-

---

*We defined success through a formula that reflects the ratio of value added over successive financing rounds divided by the initial premoney valuation of the company, corrected by the quarterly Nasdaq index. Thus, companies that provided a positive return on investment will have a positive success ratio. A success ratio of 1 indicates a 100 percent return on investment, a ratio of 2 indicates a 200 percent return on investment, etc.

† We "curved" the success ratio calculations by removing the few companies whose success ratios were in excess of 100 or below –100.

Figure F-3: Success Ratio by Initial Lead

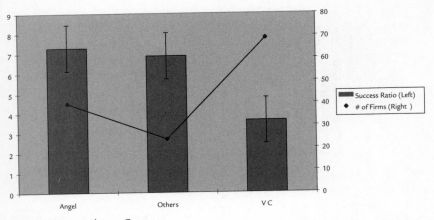

Source: PricewaterhouseCoopers

creases in value from initial financing through the end of our study period than companies that received their initial lead round of financing from other sources.*

As Figure F-4 indicates, the companies we studied availed themselves of a variety of nonfinancial investor services. The most sought after services were assistance with developing strategy, forming strategic alliances, and acquiring customers. Of the industries we looked at, semiconductor companies on average received the least nonfinancial assistance from their investors.

VC or Angel—The Impact of Initial Lead Investors

As Figure F-1 indicates, most companies in the study sample had venture capital firms or angels as initial lead investors. It makes

---

*Determining whether this is due to an artifact of the sample size (we had success data on about seventy VC-funded firms, about forty angel-funded firms, and about twenty-five firms funded by other sources) or to a trend in the industry is an interesting subject for further study.

Figure F-4: Investor Nonfinancial Assistance, by Industry

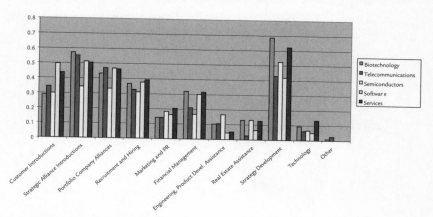

Source: PricewaterhouseCoopers

sense to examine the impact of that choice as it relates to specific value axes and to value creation overall. Before proceeding, however, we must remind readers of the hazards of aggregating data from different industry types. R&D-intensive firms are, in many respects, quite different from service-oriented companies. To mitigate those hazards, we limited our analysis in this section to software companies—the industry group that provided the largest number of cases—and divided them into two categories: companies that received lead investor funding in their seed or A round from venture capital firms (Star Chart F-1) and companies that received it from angels (Star Chart F-2).

Both groups began with favorable competitive positions. However, angel-funded companies tended to show more growth along the business model axis and on average tended to achieve superior cash flows by the B round. Management team strength grew steadily for both types of firm. With regard to performance categories, angel-funded companies significantly outpaced VC-backed companies along the product development, channels/ alliances, and customer acquisition value axes. By the time of the

Star-Chart F-1: Venture Capital

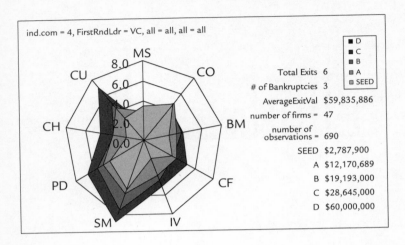

ind.com = 4, FirstRndLdr = VC, all = all, all = all

Total Exits	6
# of Bankruptcies	3
AverageExitVal	$59,835,886
number of firms =	47
number of observations =	690
SEED	$2,787,900
A	$12,170,689
B	$19,193,000
C	$28,645,000
D	$60,000,000

Star Chart F-2: Angel Funding

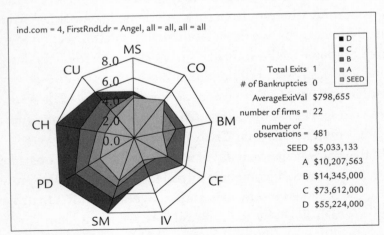

ind.com = 4, FirstRndLdr = Angel, all = all, all = all

Total Exits	1
# of Bankruptcies	0
AverageExitVal	$798,655
number of firms =	22
number of observations =	481
SEED	$5,033,133
A	$10,207,563
B	$14,345,000
C	$73,612,000
D	$55,224,000

Source: PricewaterhouseCoopers

Note: MS = market size; CP = competitive position; BM = business model; CF = cash flow; IV = investor value contributed; SM = strength of management team; PD = product development; CH = channel alliances; CU = customer acquisition

C round, however, VC-funded firms caught up and exceeded an-gel-backed firms on the customer acquisition axis.*

Software Firms by Type of Lead Investor in Seed and/or A Round

While it is impossible in the present study to ascribe a cause and effect relationship between value creation and choice of initial lead investor, the preceding charts do indicate that these two company groups developed along very different Paths to Value. Specifically:

- VC-backed companies indicated higher levels of investor contribution during the later rounds, as would be expected from full-time professional investors.

- Angel-backed companies had substantial advantages on the channels/alliances and product development performance axes, while the VC-backed companies focused more on customers.

- By the B round, angel-backed companies had outpaced VC-backed companies on all strategy axes (market size, competitive position, and business model) and were more focused on revenue and on cash flow management. The VC-backed companies had slightly better management teams at the same stage.

- Among the factors considered, market size made a major difference. Over time, VC-backed companies focused on increasingly smaller market segments, while angel-led companies focused on larger markets.

- Both groups seem to occupy similar competitive positions, but angel-backed companies used stronger channels to assert their market positions.

---

*As this finding might be the result of our sample, we do not state it as being uni-versally true.

Satisfaction with Venture Capital Investors

Overall, an average of 17 percent of managers we interviewed said that in a capital-rich environment they would not go back to the VC firms they had previously used. Given a choice, services and software company managers were least likely to use their VC investors again. Managers of R&D-oriented companies (biotech, telecoms, and semiconductors) were less likely to express this level of dissatisfaction.

Using correlation and univariate (simple) regression analysis, we were unable to establish a clear statistical relationship between a company's willingness to use its VC again and that company's level of success. This was equally true for the entire sample as for any industry group analyzed.

Figures F-5 and F-6 indicate the level of manager satisfaction with their VCs for the companies we surveyed. The data are organized by industry and by investor type, respectively.

Figure F-5: Would Not Use VC Investor Again, by Industry

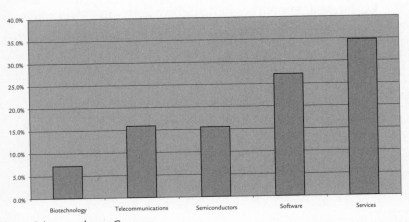

Source: PricewaterhouseCoopers

Figure F-6: Percentage of Respondent Companies That Would Not Use Lead Investor Again, by Investor Type

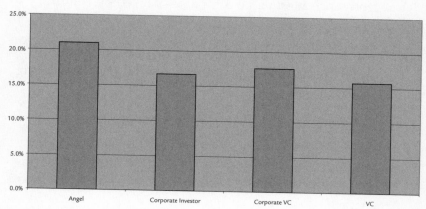

Source: PricewaterhouseCoopers

Conclusion: Key Findings

Companies relied on their investors for a variety of nonfinancial services, particularly during the early stages of financing:

- During the period of our study, companies whose initial lead investors were venture capital firms tended to increase value less successfully than companies that received their initial round of financing from other sources. The reasons why are unclear. We surmise that access to larger amounts of capital may have delayed the accomplishment of revenue, business model, and channels/alliances milestones.

- Companies backed by venture capital indicated higher levels of investor contribution during later rounds of financing. Such levels of involvement are typical of full-time, professional investors.

- Angel-backed companies gained substantial advantage along the channels/alliances and product development performance axes, while companies backed by venture capital focused more on customers.

- The most sought-after investor services were customer introductions and help in developing strategy and forming strategic alliances.

- Companies that chose venture capital firms for their lead investors traveled along different Paths to Value than did companies that chose angel investors; the former focused more on direct customer sales than channels and developed revenue later.

SURVEY CONCLUSIONS

The Paths to Value model uncovers a great deal about how early-stage companies operating under different market conditions in a variety of industries and regions have attempted to create value. In this round of research, we used the model to attempt to determine developmental strategies associated with success and failure. The results of our efforts are a number of significant insights into the value-creation impact of industries, regions, market timing, and investor roles. More important, however, we believe that the Paths to Value model will evolve from its current function as a diagnostic tool into a reliable indicator of best practices in early-stage value creation.

Using the Paths to Value model, we attempted to measure progress along nine different axes, using survey measurements at each financing event. Combined with survey valuation data, this provided diagrams of value creation, as measured by increases in value at each financing round. These nine value axes were equally distributed among three macrocategories: strategy, resources, and performance. While our company analyses with respect to these categories and their related value axes yielded considerable insight into the value-creation process, we discovered that the Paths to Value for any company could not be determined solely by its score on any given value axis at any given financing round. However, the most successful companies tended to demonstrate a balance of progress across the axes in general, particularly in terms of product development, cash flow, and business model. Even so, this balance was significantly affected by differences in industry, region, and investor role.

Axes of Value: Strategy

The three value axes that relate to a company's strategic situation are market size, competitive position, and business model.

Conclusions

- **Market Size:** An interesting finding of the report is that larger markets, whether actual or perceived, at the seed and A rounds are not necessarily an advantage. Some unsuccessful companies reported very high estimates of market size and raised significant amounts of money in an attempt to penetrate these allegedly large markets. Companies that initially focused on smaller markets often achieved lower scores on this axis, but nevertheless were able to manage growth and add more value over time.

- **Competitive Position:** The competitive position of the companies studied became clear when we compared software firms that had raised more than $20 million with those that had not. The companies that grew along this axis from the seed to A rounds of financing were able to raise higher levels of funding. In addition, in R&D-intensive industries, the more successful firms maintained scores in the 4 to 5 range, while less successful firms saw their scores on this axis decline. In software and services, most firms saw their scores decline as competition increased in their markets over time.

- **Business Model:** The comparison noted just above also illustrated the importance of the business model axis, in that it measured whether or not companies had demonstrated an ability to sell at economies of scale. During our study period, the most successful software companies, and particularly the non-U.S. software successes, showed progress along the business model axis. They had developed pricing models and demonstrated economies of scale leading to profitability.

Axes of Value: Resources

The second group of value axes—cash flow, investor value contributed, and strength of management team—reflects the resources available to each company

Conclusions

- **Cash Flow:** The importance of the cash flow axis was demonstrated through comparisons of software and services companies. The most successful of these demonstrated strong growth along this axis.

- **Investor Value Contributed:** Interpreting data along this axis was a complex process. Some troubled companies received additional nonpecuniary assistance from investors during later rounds of financing. But in general, stronger investor roles in the seed and A rounds helped distinguish the more successful from the less successful companies.

In R&D-intensive industries such as telecom and semiconductor, where major growth and successful exits are usually based on strategic deals with channel partners, nonpecuniary investor involvement increased in later rounds.

- **Strength of Management Team:** One of the most interesting findings regarding this axis was that the experience and completeness of a company's management team had a very positive impact on success in later rounds. However, complete teams at seed stages did not register as an advantage and were in fact most common during the market bubble.

Axes of Value: Performance

The last three axes concern company performance, which we measured according to product development, channels/alliances, and customer acquisition. Analysis of this value axis yielded several especially interesting findings.

Conclusions

- **Product Development:** At any given stage of financing, successful R&D-intensive firms focused less on product development than successful service-intensive firms. This finding confirmed our initial hypothesis that capital-intensive manufacturers took longer than their service-intensive counterparts to move from alpha to beta, to working versions of their products. Surprisingly, we also found that for R&D-intensive firms a high score on this axis did not always indicate success. Rather, on average, successful companies showed steady growth along this axis in parallel with progress on the customer acquisition value axis. The scores of unsuccessful companies were higher early on, but did not increase much over time. Such a finding often indicates R&D restarts and suggests that some technology-driven ventures get ahead of themselves with respect to customer and market validation.

- **Channels/Alliances and Customer Acquisition:** Concerning the small number of companies in our sample that exited as acquisitions rather than as initial public offerings, we found that channels/alliances and customer acquisition were not equally important. These companies had established a small but focused set of channel relationships that produced customers, and a number of them were acquired by their major market partners. However, the success formula varied for the independent, ongoing firms in our sample. For example, successful U.S. software companies relied on direct sales to customers, while their European counterparts achieved success by developing channels and alliances.

The Next Step: Following the Smoke to the Fire

While the above findings are of real importance, we have not yet reached the point at which we can use the Paths to Value model to specify best practices for managers of and investors in early-stage companies. We anticipate that additional research will enable us to do so. Furthermore, we cannot at this point affirm with certainty that progress along different value axes *causes* increases in valuation. While we can assert that *valuation and progress move together* in particular ways, as yet we can only surmise that this movement causes changes in valuation. A definite, provable determination of cause and effect awaits further analysis.

Even with these caveats firmly placed before the reader, we trust you will agree that the results of this report are promising.

They demonstrate that further inquiry and additional research are likely to bring us closer to clearer correlations and best practices. We are committed to following the smoke to the fire. Meanwhile, we hope to have shed substantial light on the factors affecting the valuation of private equity startups. We hope to have contributed a model and associated language that helps to clarify the experience of early-stage ventures. And we hope to have designed and effectively offered our readers a diagnostic tool that provides significant insight into various venture-development scenarios. As a concept and analytic practice in support of public scrutiny and discussion, the Paths to Value model should be able to help all participants and observers toward a deeper understanding of early-stage value creation.

HOW DOES YOUR COMPANY COMPARE?

Readers who are interested in determining how their companies compare to those in our sample will find it worthwhile to log onto the companion Web site to this report (www.pathstovalue.com). Visitors to the site can answer the same questions we posed to our survey respondents. On this basis, the Web site can manufacture a Star Chart for any company, thus enabling comparison to average values of companies at various stages of financing. As the Paths to Value series develops, we hope to be able to provide more levels of detail so as to make possible comparisons that are relevant to any company at any stage of development.

The Web site also contains contact information for PricewaterhouseCoopers consultants who can help companies gauge their performance with respect to competitors and provide assistance in making the right strategic decisions.

Appendix 2: A Brief Primer
on Venture Financing

We present here a brief overview of the process of early-stage and venture capital financing for readers who may wish to refresh their understanding of the somewhat esoteric world of private equity.

TURNING IDEAS INTO REALITY

A startup company or venture begins with an idea: a founding entrepreneur decides to create a business that will market a new product or service. Generally, the entrepreneur does not have the money necessary to build a factory and manufacture the product and has no team of specialists on hand to deliver a new service. Some entrepreneurs will draft friends and family as investors, and perhaps persuade a wealthy individual to risk investment in the new idea in return for an equity (ownership) stake in the company. Often, this angel funding will be sufficient to develop a prototype or to help the company through the first stages of development. Other entrepreneurs will receive this seed capital from venture capital firms (funds that specialize in early-stage funding), from existing corporations with an interest in developing a product outside of their internal R&D division, or even from an "incubator," an organization set up to provide assistance, office space, and advice to entrepreneurs. The impact of early investors on the Paths to Value is an understudied topic that forms a key focus of this report.

FINANCING ROUNDS

To survive, the new company will need additional infusions of cash. Often, a new company will go through several rounds of financing. Traditionally, the round after the seed round is called the A round, followed by the B round, and so on. Depending on the industry, firm characteristics, and the market environment, companies may go through numerous rounds of financing.

At each financing event, investors estimate the value of the company and additional capital is added to that value. As an example, consider a software company that has developed an interesting application but needs to hire programmers and sales associates and to develop a marketing plan. If the company is valued at $1 million, and a venture capitalist adds an infusion equal to that amount, the investors then own 50 percent of the company (which, after the transaction, would be valued at $2 million). Over time, the company could grow and develop to the point where it might be worth many millions of dollars. The investors' 50 percent ownership, however, remains in place unless the VC firm decides to sell that ownership interest to another party. To maximize their ownership stakes, venture capitalists naturally prefer to contribute funds at low valuations. Prestigious VC firms are often able to negotiate low valuations at various rounds of financing. However, at the point when these firms desire to sell their portion of the company, they are interested in obtaining very high valuations. This dynamic complicates the measurement of private company value. (For purposes of this analysis, we split the sample into two groups and did not mix valuations of companies that remain private and independent with those that have gone public or have been acquired by other companies.)

EXIT

Eventually the new company outgrows the startup label and exits this status in a number of ways. In a difficult market environment, a company may declare bankruptcy. If it does, its worth then corresponds to the market value of the assets liquidated (after creditors, if any, have been compensated).

Another possibility is that the company will be acquired. Mergers and acquisitions are a desirable exit option for a large number of companies that otherwise would be unable to survive on their own.

A third option—one that fueled the Internet bubble—is for the company to survive as an independent, ongoing concern. The decision to exit the world of private equity financing and to access public capital markets is a difficult one. Going the initial public offering (IPO) route requires that the company incur the significant expensive of registering with the Securities and Exchange Commission, find an investment banker to underwrite the shares, determine the right share price, and locate a pool of investors interested in purchasing the company's shares. Entrepreneurs and investors whose companies reach this stage of development often acquire significant wealth through a successful IPO.

Appendix 3: Survey Sample and Methodology

SAMPLE

In preparing this report, we contacted more than 400 companies, of which more than 350 generously agreed to share with us detailed information about their experiences in the private equity market. In a large number of cases, this information concerned all nine axes of value for a given firm in every major financing event the company underwent. In the end, we collected detailed data on 162 firms in the United States, 87 in the United Kingdom, and 102 companies located in other countries in Europe and in Israel. In addition to questions related to the axes of value, we asked questions that provided important background information on the perceptions of early-stage companies. These data have been compiled into the various charts and figures that can be found throughout the report.

The Star Charts typically represent a number of companies and capture several data points (observations) for each financing round and each axis of value. The number of observations ranges from a low of 109 to a high of 847, with the average being between 400 and 500 (depending on the industry and the criteria used to parse the data). Each layer or financing round may reflect a slightly different makeup of underlying firms, based on the availability of data. In general, seed and A round financings reflect more companies than C round financing.

COMPANY PROFILE

We sourced all of the companies in this study from the Venture-One database and included companies from the biopharmaceutical, telecommunications and optical, electronics and semiconductors, and software and services industries. We downloaded data from VentureOne in September 2001.

We asked the majority of companies in the sample for an interview at least once, and many were contacted as often as four times.

SELECTION CRITERIA

The companies in the study received their first round of financing either during or after 1999.

PARTICIPANT SELECTION

In each case, our interviews were conducted with senior executives (CEOs, CFOs, or chairmen) listed as such in the VentureOne database.

METHODOLOGY

The interviews were conducted by telephone from the PricewaterhouseCoopers International Survey Unit based in Belfast, Northern Ireland.

INTERVIEWER QUALIFICATIONS

All interviewers meet the IQCS (Interviewer Quality Control Scheme) standard, which is the industry standard for quality fieldwork. The interviewers are skilled in financial services and business-to-business research and have been involved in numerous surveys of this type. All interviews were conducted in accordance with the MRS (Market Research Society) Code of Conduct, which guarantees the interviewees total anonymity and confidentiality.

INTERVIEWING DATES

The interviews took place from September 28 to December 10, 2001. Most interviews took place during October 2001.

Appendix 4: Definitions of Performance Categories and Axes of Value

In this study, we analyzed company development over time from the perspective of three broad categories: strategy, performance, and resources. In addition, to each of these categories, we assigned three axes of value.

STRATEGY

This category measures the company's strategic situation in three major areas:

- **Market Size (MS):** Measurements on this value axis were determined by answers to the following questions: How large was the projected market size for the company's product? Did the company perform detailed marketing studies to arrive at this estimate? A score of 1 on this axis indicates that no marketing studies were carried out. A higher score indicates that the company had carried out or commissioned a professional marketing study and that the market size for its product exceeded several billion dollars.

- **Competitive Position (CP):** This axis measures the level of the company's competition. A low score indicates that the company was facing stiff competition from a variety of well-funded rivals; a high score indicates solid patent protection and no reliance on first-mover advantage.

- **Business Model (BM):** Measurement on this value axis was determined by the answer to the following question: How well thought out was the company's business model and how well was it validated with consistent sales patterns, pricing models, and evidence of economies of scale? A score of 1 indicates that the company did not have a pricing model. A higher score indicates that the company had sold product/services and demonstrated economies of scale and also that it had significant quarterly revenues (in excess of $10,000).

RESOURCES

This category measures three types of resources that companies draw upon in order to create value:

- **Cash Flow (CF):** Measurement on this value axis was determined by the answer to the following question: Did the company's revenue stream outpace its burn rate? Cash flow break-even is indicated by a score of 7.

- **Investor Value Contributed (IV):** This value axis focused on the active role investors played during various stages of the ventures and on how important entrepreneurs believed this assistance to be with respect to the success of the company.

- **Strength of Management Team (SM):** This value axis had a huge impact on value and company success, but this impact varied immensely over the study period. For example, during the bubble companies easily attracted complete, experienced management teams very early in the life of the company.

PERFORMANCE

The third category examines three performance metrics:

- **Channels/Alliances (C/A):** Measurements on this value axis were determined by the answer to the following question: What was the status of the company's partnerships and channel alliances at any given stage of financing? A score of 1 indicates that the company had no alliances. A high score indicates that the company had channel and alliance deals that significantly contributed to revenue.

- **Customer Acquisition (CA):** Measurement on this value axis was determined by the answer to the following question: How many paying customers did the company have at any given financing event? A score of 1 indicates that the company had no customers. Companies with trial (though paying) customers scored in the middle of this axis. Companies with very high scores had a pipeline and several quarters of growth.

- **Product Development (PD):** Measurement on this value axis was determined by the answer to the following question: How developed was the product? High scores on this axis were given to companies that had developed working versions of their products or had executed multiple releases of multiple products. Companies that had gotten only as far as a conceptual or alpha version of their products received low scores.

Subsequent Round Funding Versus
No Subsequent Funding, as of June 2003

The following Star Chart comparisons designate companies as either X Group or Y Group. X Group companies received a new round of funding after the initial survey (June 2001 through September 2002). Y Group companies received no subsequent funding during that period. The analyses are presented collectively, by industry, and by geography.

Collective Grouping
Funding Round
Seed Round
A Round
B Round
C Round
D Round

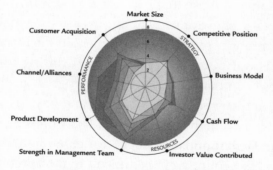

X Group = 135 companies

Source: PricewaterhouseCoopers

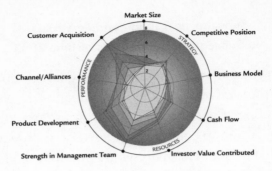

Y Group = 216 companies

Source: PricewaterhouseCoopers

In total, 38 percent of the original 351 companies achieved a subsequent round of funding after June 2001 (if just the 328 companies still in business as of the follow-up in 2002 are considered, then the rate is 41 percent). These X Group companies did better in terms of their business models and channel alliances than Y Group companies—those that had not obtained further funding. The X Group also shows an advantage in cash flow in the B and D rounds, and stronger product development in the D round. The Y Group stands out in customer acquisition during the C and D rounds. These companies make steady progress in building on the strength of their management teams and have a superior position in that regard in the final rounds. The Y Group also derived greater value in all rounds from investor value contributed.

Data examined collectively is difficult to interpret because the process of combining data tends to hide differences that may be noticeable when specific criteria are examined—for example, by industry or geography. Starker contrasts emerge as the data is examined with greater granularity, i.e., by industry and geographically.

Telecom

X Group = 35 companies

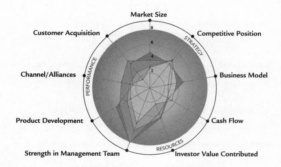

Y Group = 24 companies

Source: PricewaterhouseCoopers

Fifty-nine percent of telecom companies in the study were able to obtain additional funding, making this industry group the most successful. These firms did better in the majority of the categories during the C round: channel/alliances, customer acquisition, cash flow, product development, and investor value contributed.

Semiconductors

X Group = 21 companies

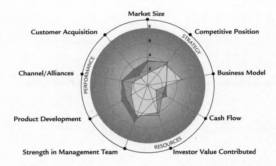

Y Group = 16 companies

Source: PricewaterhouseCoopers

Semiconductors were the second most successful group in terms of obtaining additional funding, with 57 percent of these firms achieving a subsequent round. This group, like telecom, scored better in the majority of categories. It shows consistently stronger scores through all rounds for strength in management teams and demonstrates an advantage in cash flow, business model, customer acquisition, and investor value contributed during the B round. The semiconductor group also started out in the seed round with a significant advantage, scoring higher in seven of the nine axes of value (all but business model and investor value contributed).

Biotech

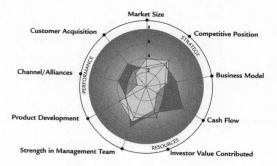

X Group = 18 companies

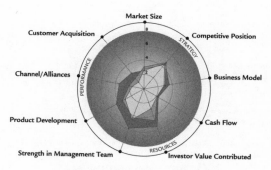

Y Group = 42 companies

Source: PricewaterhouseCoopers

Thirty percent of the biotech firms in the study received a subsequent round of funding. They scored higher than the Y Group in customer acquisition during seed, A, and B rounds and in cash flow during A and B rounds. At the seed round, these firms had stronger performance in terms of product development, market size, strength of management team, and investor value contributed. They also demonstrated stronger business models during the B round.

Software

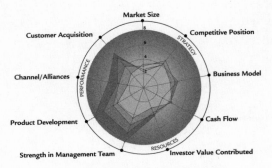

X Group = 31 companies

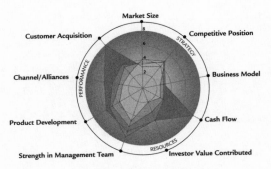

Y Group = 48 companies

Source: PricewaterhouseCoopers

Two axes of value stand out with regard to the software industry group, which had a 39 percent success rate: Companies obtaining new rounds of funding scored consistently higher with respect to business model, while those that did not obtain a new round had a consistently better score in their estimate of the market size. Product development was also key for X Group companies, which scored better during seed, A, and C rounds. The B round score for product development was the same for both X Group companies and Y Group companies. X Group companies also had better cash flow scores in the seed through B rounds, but the Y Group stands out in cash flow as well as in customer acquisition during the C round. This fact could indicate that for these companies, customers and a steady cash flow could have precluded the need to seek an additional funding round.

Services

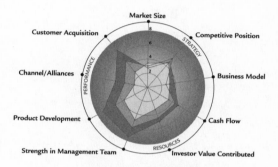

X Group = 28 companies

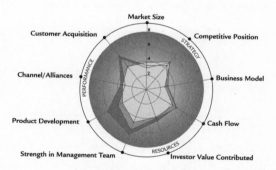

Y Group = 61 companies

Source: PricewaterhouseCoopers

Services firms achieved a 31 percent funding rate and these X Group companies achieved higher scores in the B round on six of nine axes: customer acquisition, channel/alliances, product development, strength of management team, investor value contributed, and business model. The Y Group, however, started in the seed round with advantages in customer acquisition, channel/ alliances, investor value contributed, and competitive position. At the seed round, the only advantage for the X Group was in business model. At 31 percent, services companies are also near the bottom of the success rate for achieving funding.

By Region

United States

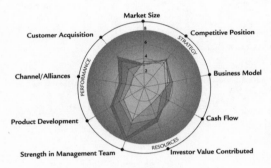

X Group = 61 companies

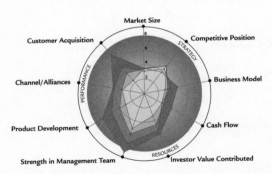

Y Group = 101 companies

Source: PricewaterhouseCoopers

Thirty-eight percent of U.S. companies obtained a new round of funding. Very little distinguished the X Group among the U.S. companies. They do score higher in competitive position in the B and C rounds, in business model for seed and B rounds, and in product development during the seed round. The companies that did not obtain a new round do, however, show clear distinction in cash flow and in channel alliances throughout all the rounds. They also have stronger scores in six of the nine categories for the C round, for customer acquisition in A and C rounds, and for investor value contributed in seed, B, and C rounds. Again, it is possible that a better cash flow position precludes the necessity for seeking additional rounds of funding.

United Kingdom

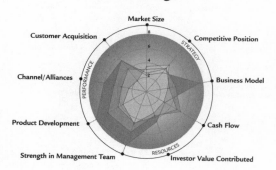

X Group = 34 companies

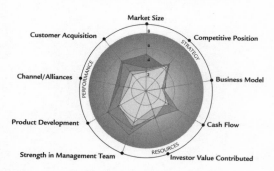

Y Group = 55 companies

Source: PricewaterhouseCoopers

In the United Kingdom, 38 percent of the companies in this group also obtained a subsequent round of funding. However, a number of patterns emerge with regard to the X Group of U.K. companies. Business model scores are higher in all the rounds and scores for channel/alliances are higher in rounds A through C. U.K. companies that received subsequent funding also scored higher in customer acquisition at A and B rounds, product development and strength of management at C round, and market size and investor value contributed at the seed round.

Europe and Israel

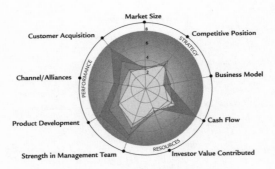

X Group = 40 companies

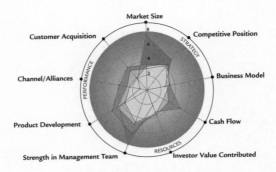

Y Group = 60 companies

Source: PricewaterhouseCoopers

Europe and Israel (Excluding the United Kingdom)

Forty percent of the European and Israeli companies obtained additional funding. They scored higher during the C round in all categories but market size and competitive position (seven out of nine). They also showed an advantage in customer acquisition during seed, B and C rounds, in channel/alliances during A and C rounds, in product development during seed and C rounds, in strength of management team during seed, A, and C rounds, and in cash flow during seed and C rounds. Market size, which was consistently stronger for the Y Group companies for all rounds, was not a factor for these companies.

Index

Akamai
  board of directors of, 57, 66–69
  cash flow of, 77–78
  Conrades as CEO of, 22, 27,
    51–55, 66–67, 69, 77–78, 141, 182
  Coyne as lead director of, 59,
    66–69, 128, 131, 138–39, 158, 177
  exit strategy of, 18
  growth of, 27, 53–54
  Internet/NASDAQ bubble and,
    22–24, 141
  management team of, 53–55
Alliances. *See* Channels/alliances
Angel investors
  on boards of directors, 56–57,
    64–65
  Internet/NASDAQ bubble and, 34
  role of, 2, 5, 56, 92–93, 142–43,
    168, 203, 264
  VCs v., 250–54*f*, 250–58, 257*f*

Bankruptcy, 266
Benchmarking, 80, 125–26
Bernal, Ron, 99–100, 162, 181
  interview with, 90–94
Biotech firms, 277*f*

Boards of directors
  CEOs working with, 152
  Internet/NASDAQ bubble's
    influence on, 56–58
  investors on, 56–59, 63–71, 150,
    152, 182
  as management's partner, 70–71,
    152
  priorities for choosing, 7, 152
  role of, 7, 25, 54–55, 62–69, 182
  value created by, 64–65, 182
Branding, 100–101, 110–11, 134–35,
  182
Burn rate, 10, 72, 75–76, 82, 143
Business developers, 143–44, 169,
  176–77
Business models, 24, 26, 34–36, 83,
  106, 114–16, 123–24, 129, 132,
  185, 196–204, 209–10, 220–33,
  235–44, 253–55, 257–60
  benchmarking for, 125–26
  cash flow generated by, 74, 80, 128
  creation of, 120–22, 124
  definition of, 116, 271
  evolution of, 124, 126–28, 177
  of Google, 126